No
Margin
for Error

America in the

No.
Eighties Margin for Error

Senator Howard Baker

Introduction by
Senator Daniel Patrick Moynihan

Times BOOKS

Published by TIMES BOOKS, a division of
Quadrangle/The New York Times Book Co., Inc.,
Three Park Avenue, New York, N.Y. 11016

Published simultaneously in Canada by
Fitzhenry & Whiteside, Ltd., Toronto

Library of Congress Cataloging in Publication Data

Baker, Howard Henry, 1925–
No margin for error.

1. United States—Politics and government—1945–
2. United States—Economic policy—1971–
3. United States—Foreign relations—1945—
4. United States—Politics and government—1977–
5. Presidents—United States—Election—1980.
I. Title.
E839.5.B35 1980   973.926   79-91670
ISBN 0-8129-0900-3

Manufactured in the United States of America

To my father, Howard H. Baker, Sr., to my stepmother, Irene Baker, and to my father-in-law, Everett McKinley Dirksen. By precept and example they inculcated in me the firm and lasting belief that politics is an honorable undertaking and that public service is among the highest callings open to members of the human society.

Introduction

As the 1980 Presidential year began, David Broder commented on what may prove its most enduring and surely least anticipated aspect: Republicans had become, or were becoming, the party of ideas. He wrote of the Republican National Committee under the direction of its effervescent chairman Bill Brock of Tennessee:

> It has moved heavily into the issues area, in preparation for the 1980 platform debates, and is publishing the most lively political party journals since the days of the *Democratic Digest* under Paul Butler 20 years ago.*

That certainly is the only possible analogy that provides a reasonable measure of comparison; but, as a veteran of those years in the 1950's when the Democratic National Committee was a lively center of political opposition, I would suggest that it is not really adequate. It does not really describe what has come over the Republicans.

Take, for example, the *Democratic Digest* which first appeared in 1953 and continued publication to 1961; the pe-

---

* David S. Broder, "From the Grass Roots Up," *The Washington Post,* January 23, 1980.

riod, that is, of a Republican administration. While it was certainly a provocative publication, it lacked many of the qualities that we now see in comparable Republican journals. Part of the problem was that it was in opposition as much to the Democratic leadership of the Congress as to the Republican President in the White House. But more importantly, it celebrated—and took for granted—the established ideas of the time without, in Lionel Trilling's plea at the time, putting any pressure on them. It was really not much more than a practice manual for the preparation of Presidential Messages to Congress in the decade that followed.

Contrast *Commonsense*, "A Republican Journal of Thought and Opinion" which first appeared in 1978 with the Chairman of the Republican National Committee as Publisher. The members of its editorial board—Peter L. Berger, Fred C. Ikle, Paul McCracken, Laurence H. Silberman, Herbert Stein, and Ralph Winter, Jr.—comprise as distinguished a body of academics and working intellectuals as is associated with any contemporary publication.

The journal's expressed goal?—to question the orthodoxies of the time, providing a forum for the testing and refining of established ideas and the articulation of new thought. Indeed, it is in this willingness to challenge established ideas that *Commonsense* succeeds where the *Democratic Digest* failed. But could this questioning of the status quo possibly be the policy of a *Republican* journal? Just so. Herewith Publisher Brock in an opening statement of the first issue:

> It is said of political parties that they exist to contest elections. That is, in fact, what we do. But that is not all that can be said about the Republican Party. To complete the description, it is necessary to know what we are, and how we are perceived by ourselves and by others. The distance now separating what we think of ourselves and what we are thought to be by the public at large poses a problem of significant dimension.
>
> Rather than essential links between individuals and

their government, political parties today are viewed widely as the instruments of special interest. Party politics is often regretted, as if in America some other kind of politics were desirable. Parties have been, but are perceived to be less so now, the credible communicators of political information and the sponsors of candidates and programs which represent a coherent set of ideas. These candidates and programs and ideas were to do the battle of politics, engaging in the contests for votes. But much of what we were or should be has been taken from us or yielded by us to other institutions—government not the least among them.

In the current context then, it may be that this Republican Journal of Thought and Opinion, COMMON-SENSE, goes against the "common wisdom," and that the publication of such a Journal will be unexpected and in some quarters, suspect.

However, it is the first principle of politics, wrote the Englishman G. K. Chesterton in *Orthodoxy,* that "the essential things in men are the things they hold in common, not the things they hold separately." Political parties in America do not propose "orthodoxies," they have served as structures for conducting that search for the things we hold in common. They should be vehicles for discovering the common sense of Americans about themselves and their institutions.

If they are not, then the American public faces the alternative of being exposed to a continuing parade of untested ideas. And these ideas can be imposed on a public unconvinced of their merits, but without the mechanisms to refine or resist them. This alternative, COMMONSENSE rejects. Rather, for the Republican Party, this Journal is intended to be one of those mechanisms.

We must not forget that the last great partisan coalition of American politics was built on ideas. These were no less forceful and appealing, if also debatable, for all their identification with a political party. The notion of an activist federal government, with an obligation to use its centralized power "to meet new social problems with new social controls," was a new idea in the 1930s. But it took hold, built a durable coalition, became the foundation for decades of programmatic public policy, and tended to capture the terms of the political debate.

As an idea, it had consequences. Only lately have these come to be generally understood as having mixed implications for the nation and for individuals in it. Accordingly, the Republican Party finds itself in opposition, at this writing, not only to a majority party that controls the machineries of government, but to the force of certain such ideas. It is our continuing obligation, therefore, in COMMONSENSE and elsewhere, to articulate our own.*

And so they have done under the superb leadership of editor Michael E. Baroody. Indeed, they have pursued their course with such effect that, in the Fall of 1979, Jeane Kirkpatrick—perhaps the most formidable intellectual we Democrats have going for us just now—felt compelled to write for *Commonsense* an essay entitled "Why We Don't Become Republicans."

What's going on here? This I think essential. The Republican Party may not of late have been a party of ideas in America, *but it began as one* and has never wholly lost that attachment. The credit for reviving the conscious tradition must surely go to the Ripon Society, founded in 1962 in Cambridge, Massachusetts, as "the national progressive Republican research and policy organization." Taking its name from Ripon, Wisconsin, the site of the Republican Party's birth, the Ripon Society raised that old Republican standard. By the mid-1960's—as Democratic discourse became shrill to the point, at times, of incoherence—the steady, reasoned, reasonable proposals of the Ripon Society attracted more atten-

* Bill Brock, "Introduction to a Republican Journal of Thought and Opinion," *Commonsense,* Summer, 1978, pp. iii-iv.

tion, much in the manner of a soft-spoken trial lawyer whom juries strain to hear.

The *Ripon Forum*, now in its fifteenth year of publication, is a quality journal. But more important is the fact that there is no equivalent to either the *Ripon Forum* or *Commonsense* within the Democratic Party.

It is revealing that the circulation literature of the *Ripon Forum* features an endorsement from Howard H. Baker, Jr. As minority leader of the United States Senate he is to be judged the highest ranking Republican official in the national government. The impressive fact is that when he is quoted in the literature as saying he has read the *Forum* for years, it is true, and it is equally true for any number of journals of his own party. Indeed, Senator Baker is very much a man of ideas—new ideas—as *No Margin for Error* will make abundantly clear to any who share such taste, or to the no doubt larger number who are skeptical that a working politician should do so.

Let it be clear that he is first of all just that—a working politician. He writes:

> I've spent most of my life as a politician. I guess some people would call me an "insider." (That generally means that you have some idea of how things happen and why; and how to change the mix when it's necessary to get the right mix and get good results.) As long as I can remember, I've been around men and women who lived and breathed politics and policy. To be a politician should be a source of enormous pride to those who are lucky enough to be in public life.

Baker's love of politics reflects a streak of honest family pride. The Baker's are from Tennessee, where more than most places politics go back generations. Scott County sided with the Union during the Civil War and stayed Republican in the generations that followed. His grandmother, "Mother Ladd" to him, was Sheriff of the county. His father repre-

sented the district in the United States House of Representatives from the 82nd to the 88th Congress. Upon his father's
death, his stepmother, Irene Bailey Baker, served the balance
of the unexpired term. He, himself, married Joy, the gracious
and talented daughter of Senator Everett McKinley Dirksen
of Illinois.

As he relates in the present volume, he had no thoughts
of politics until his father died and Estes Kefauver's seat
in the Senate suddenly became available. He won the Republican Senate nomination with surprising ease and, as
he recounts, seemed on his way to election when Senator
Barry Goldwater, running for President, arrived in Knoxville. After being introduced by Baker, Senator Goldwater
promptly offered to sell the Tennessee Valley Authority—a
proposal that, needless to say, did not exactly thrill the
Knoxville crowd—and Baker accordingly watched his Senate
aspirations "go down the drain."

I was then an Assistant Secretary of Labor in the Johnson
Administration and would probably never have taken notice
of the incident had not Fred Graham—a Tennessee Democrat of considerable conviction—reported it to me with
measured satisfaction. So, in the manner of archeologists, we
may assert with some confidence that Howard Baker's interest in political ideas began no later than that day in 1964 in
the Knoxville airport. It was well established when. two
years later, he was elected to the Senate.

Now, after 13 effective years in the United States Senate,
Howard Baker's political ideas—merely nascent at Knoxville
—have been richly developed. I have been asked as a colleague to write an Introduction to his book and I am honored to do so. The reader will have no difficulty following
the ideas and arguments expressed in this insightful work,
set forth as they are in a succession of succinct and orderly
chapters. I do not write to endorse them—indeed I do not
endorse them. I write to urge that they be given a hearing

as the thoughts of an experienced, reflective man devoted to his nation and his party.

Still, it would be ungracious not to call attention to a particularly rich vein in this book, that being Baker's persistent interest in the *process* of American government. In the Senate it is much of his life; he and the majority leader keep the institution running smoothly. It is the single commanding insight of our political tradition—and never to be underestimated—that where there are only ideas and no process, whirl is king. Baker recognizes this. He is at his best in commenting on the voids that now separate the three branches of the federal government and the entropy that somehow seems to be settling upon us. "Government by stalemate" he calls it.

Citing George Will, who argues that the Presidency is an inherently weak office, he contends that the President is not the acme of power often believed—that it is merely an integral portion of the political process. He has an idea:

> I'd like to think that the next President will conclude the inaugural ceremony by opening a Presidential office in the Capitol itself, where he can deal daily and personally with the men and women who enact the laws of the land. If anything is clear about the way this government works, it is the simple fact that the President may propose, but that he risks all if he forgets that it is Congress which will dispose.

This is not the least impractical, and extraordinarily important. Professor Arthur S. Link, the biographer of Woodrow Wilson, has commented that Wilson worked well with Congress largely because of the absence of any White House staff to manage. In a sense, the only people he had to talk to *were* members of Congress, and he benefited because of it.

But for sheer insight, there is not a better passage in this book than that on the isolation of the Justices of the Supreme Court, or yet a wiser and more revealing observation than this: "I think it was a mistake that we let them move out of the Capitol, where they held court for many, many years."

It was 145 years to be exact until they moved away in 1935. It *was* a mistake and it was *our* error. (For Congress had to pass a law enabling the great marble palace where the Justices reside to be built.) Now, regrettably, we hardly ever see them and they hardly ever see us and, in the rare occasions when we do meet, our conversations become near to embarrassed as if some huge impropriety might suddenly inject itself. Howard Baker is enough of a conservative to be careful about the arrangements he changes.

Now it would be a disservice to Howard Baker and to truth to present him as some kind of Platonic sage, indifferent to public approval and incapable of folly. Many of the passages in this work are considerably more partisan than seems to me useful even to avowedly partisan purposes. At other points, his enthusiasm for the United States gets beyond the demands of patriotism. Take, for example, the following: "It's a place where hard work, good spirit, and good will have made all things possible." A true bred and honest conservative, he would do well to ponder Michael Oakeshott's well-known formulation in his inaugural lecture on acceding to Harold Laski's chair at the London School of Economics: "It is the best of all possible worlds, and everything in it is a necessary evil."

But then Howard Baker is not wholly to be held responsible for optimism. It is part of the very tradition he would conserve. Such is his prerogative. Thomas Sowell (who would, I believe, regard himself as a conservative) has written in his new book, *Knowledge and Decisions*:

> If a conservative is someone who wants to conserve,
> then what specifically he wants to conserve depends
> upon what happens to exist, and this might be anything
> from the social-political system of eighteenth-century

England to the contemporary Soviet Union. In short, the broad label "conservative" is itself virtually devoid of content, however much specific content there may be in each of the groupings and individuals to whom that label is loosely applied.*

Sowell observes, and rightly, that this has led to a condition in which it is most often liberals that define what is conservatism. It is this imbalance that Howard Baker addresses himself with authority and confidence in *No Margin for Error: America in the Eighties.*

No matter what, he will be an important American figure for the rest of the century and from across the aisle I salute him. Trusting to his unfailing good nature and good humor, I take my leave with the wish that he long remain minority leader of the United States Senate!

Daniel Patrick Moynihan

Washington, D.C.
January 27, 1980

* Thomas Sowell, *Knowledge and Decisions,* Basic Books, 1979, p. 366.

Acknowledgments

This book is an expression of the reality that public life, in its every aspect, is a collaborative enterprise. I wish, in particular, to express my deep appreciation to Don Kellermann, who gave me from the origins of this project to its conclusion, the editorial support and assistance that helped to bring it to life. The generosity of my Senate colleague, Daniel Patrick Moynihan of New York, is matched by his usual felicity of expression in the Introduction he was gracious enough to write for this volume. His thoughtful essay is a unique expression of the civility of a political tradition in which ideas may be assessed for their content without regard to the partisan labels of those who offer them. The intellectual stimulation afforded by the ideas of scholars such as Arthur Burns, Michael Boskin, professor of economics at Stanford University, and Richard Pipes, professor of history at Harvard University, is gratefully acknowledged. The Congressional Research Service of the Library of Congress and the U.S. Senate Library staff have been unfailingly courteous and efficient in providing some of the materials that illustrate the themes of my argument. Karen Pritchard performed prodigal emergency research and typing into the very closing hours of 1979. Tom Lipscomb, President of Times Books, has my thanks for suggesting that I examine the outlook for the eighties from my own perspective and experience, and for bringing these thoughts to the attention of the reading public. Finally, Joy Baker, my wife and companion for twenty-eight years, has my gratitude for her patient understanding of the requirements of the political life and her partnership in my efforts to deal with the problems discussed in these pages.

Contents

Foreword

In 1980 Americans are listening for a drum beat with a certain rhythm. We live in a continental nation with outposts on two great oceans, and we have a long history of prosperity and dynamic leadership in the good times and in times of stress as well.

We have come from every part of the globe, we Americans. That is what makes us the miracle we are. The American experiment has worked on a scale never before recorded in the annals of human accomplishment. We may be the products of a melting pot or we may be a tossed salad. Take your pick.

We live in a country in which the pursuit of happiness is enshrined as a national purpose. America has been a dream for hundreds of millions of people for nearly five hundred years. Those who made the dream into their personal reality have held a winning ticket in the human lottery. We are a nation of winners, and I believe that as individuals and as a people we have usually behaved with the generosity and the good spirit of men and women who have faith in themselves and in the meaning of their lives.

In recent years, although most of the American people continue to have confidence in their own individual fortunes, and although most of us are fully aware that we are lucky to live in a republic where freedom is the rule and not its exception, we have grown uneasy about the manner, the methods, and the failures of those we elect to represent and to lead us.

We are emerging from a decade in which much went wrong with the American experiment. We fought an unsuccessful jungle war that bitterly divided us at home; we saw a President and Vice-President driven in disgrace from the highest posts in the public service. As a result, cynicism and distrust of our institutions are dramatically on the rise.

The seventies have not been an easy time. The tremors in our society and the uncertainty of our leadership have enabled powerful adversaries in the world to grow in strength and open brutality. We have been shocked into an awareness of the vulnerability of the fuel supply that sustains our economy. And too many citizens have turned away from public life because they feel it's beyond their control.

I'm the last man in America to excuse our shortcomings. I believe in fixing them. That's what we have always done in the past, and that's what we must do as we enter the eighties. We live on an oasis of freedom and opportunity in the center of a dangerous world. We must protect its vitality. It's a place where hard work, good spirit, and goodwill have made all things possible. We must keep it that way.

This is a "how to" book. I believe that we must first understand what has gone wrong. Then we must take the specific actions that will ensure that the American Republic continues to grow and sustain its meaning as that place where hopes and dreams come true.

If we understand our problems and if we apply the solutions suggested in the pages that follow, we will do what Americans have always done: we will keep our rendezvous with destiny.

Howard Baker

January, 1980

Part I

The Politics of Policy and Process

1

Emergencies, Dogmas, and Mandarins

When I watched Jimmy Carter walk up Pennsylvania Avenue from the Capitol to the White House, I knew that we were seeing a calculated piece of symbolism that augured Carter's intention to cast himself in a new political mold. But, more than three years later, it has become apparent that there was far more to that symbolic act than either the new President or his audience understood on that brisk January day. He has isolated himself from the legislative body that bears constitutional power and responsibility equal to his own. This self-imposed isolation cut him off from the reality of a vigorous body politic that solves its problems through intense debate and the accommodation of varied and conflicting interests.

I'd like to think that the next President of the United States will begin *his* administration with another symbolic act. I'd like to think that the next President will conclude the inaugural ceremony by opening a presidential office in the Capitol itself, where he can deal daily and personally with the men and women who enact the laws of the land. If anything is clear about the way this government works, it is the simple fact that the President may propose, but that he risks all if he forgets that it is Congress which will dispose.

Columnist George Will once wrote that "the presidency is an inherently weak office, a fact that has been obscured by the accrual of extra-presidential power during the periods of national emergency that have dominated much of the twentieth century." Although I happen to believe that the presidency is as strong an office as should be held by any single man or woman, I think that George Will is onto a very important fact of life that's often missed by the professional Washington watchers, and obscured by the attention we lavish on every family who lives in the White House and every social event that occurs there. When most Americans think about Washington, the White House and the President and his family personify the city and the country itself. Foreigners have, until just recently, had the misconception that when the President lifts his finger the nation rises to do his bidding. But American Presidents over the years, and Jimmy Carter in particular, have learned that it isn't that simple. The presidency *is* a powerful office, but it's not the only game in town.

The first President of the United States was also the first President to learn that lesson. It was brought sharply home when he visited the United States Senate.

Like everything else the founders shaped, the Senate has repeatedly adapted its role to changing times. Although Alexander Hamilton thought senators should serve for life, and although the whole idea seems to have been to put a brake on popular government, the Senate has become an independent voice of the people; so independent that more than one President has wished that the Constitution had balanced the powers of government just a little bit differently.

When George Washington visited the Capitol to get the Senate to "advise and consent" on an Indian treaty he had negotiated, he tried to stack the deck a little. Washington brought along the first secretary of war, General Knox, to explain things to the full Senate. Twenty-two senators were seated in a small, intimate chamber one floor below the one we use today (the flavor of Senate time is best captured in the fact that senators have been working in the "new" chamber since 1859). As Knox read the treaty, article by article, and section by section, the first Vice-President, John Adams, tried to create a brand-new precedent for treaty ratification. Every time Knox looked up expectantly at the conclusion of a treaty article, John Adams would say in an official voice, "Do you, Senators . . . advise and consent?" But something went awry with the script. Not a senator raised his voice to "aye" or "nay." There was complete quiet in the chamber and Washington's face became gloomier by the minute. Finally, Senator Mosby of Georgia rose and moved that the treaty be referred to a committee so that it could be studied before the Senate took any action.

Senate lore has it that as Washington stormed out of the room muttering, "This defeats every purpose of my coming here," he swore, "I'll be damned if I ever again set foot in that chamber." But he was back three days later and he graciously accepted several suggestions made by the Senate after the treaty had been adequately studied. That, however, was the last time Washington or any other President officially appeared in the Capitol on presidential business, for anything but the State of the Union message. I believe that two hundred years of absence is long enough. In the 1980's we can't afford that psychological mile that separates one end of Pennsylvania Avenue from the other. The President can be sure the Congress will welcome him back.

Government is a partnership, and the President is one of the partners. If he can't use his powers with enough subtlety and enough imagination to convince Congress and to convince the bureaucracy (the fourth branch of government) that he's on the right track, he's in deep trouble and so are the American people. I believe that's the way things are today, and I believe that it's time to do something about it.

It's time to ask ourselves *What must be done?* and *How must we do it?*

I've spent much of my life as a politician. I guess some people would call me an "insider." (That generally means that you have some idea of how things happen and why; and how to change the mix when it's necessary to get good results.) As long as I can remember, I've been around men and women who lived and breathed politics and policy. To be a politician should be a source of enormous pride to those who are lucky enough to be in public life. I learned that lesson very early from my grandmother. She was "Mother Ladd" to me, but she was "Sheriff" to everyone else in the county.

I know, of course, that the great questions we face at the close of the twentieth century are very different from the problems confronted by a woman sheriff in that rural county in Tennessee over half a century ago. But I believe that the tough realism tempered with optimism that was generated by my grandmother and her neighbors, and their ancestors, and their children, are essential ingredients in our attempt to maintain continuity and to keep the system alive and healthy. It's an effort that most of us don't even think about unless we must.

In my own case I cannot recall a single, conscious thought that I was going into political life until after my father died. That may have been a subconscious judgment that one man in the family at a time was enough in politics. It may be that I avoided the competition that inevitably results. But a number of things came together at the same time. I had reached the same place in life that my father had when he first ran for Congress. I had practiced law for seventeen years. I had done pretty well financially. My family had reached the point where the children were sufficiently grown to move in a healthy kind of way. I was ready for a change. Estes Kefauver had died suddenly and his Senate seat was open.

Running for the Senate was a fascinating prospect. I recall I had no particular expectation of winning. But I thought if I was ever going to be involved in politics this was the time to dip a foot in the water. I got 48 percent of the vote, which was a great surprise to everybody, including me. It wasn't until the last two or three weeks of the campaign that it dawned on me that "You might just mess around and win this thing."

I continued to think so until the day when Barry Goldwater came to Tennessee. Barry was the Republican presidential nominee in 1964 and I was proud to introduce him from the platform at Knoxville Airport. As soon as I sat down he offered to sell the TVA! I could see my prospects going right down the drain.

I sat there on the platform wishing that, instead of introducing Goldwater, I had said, "Senator Goldwater has asked me to say a few words on his behalf."

Barry and I have become close friends but I will always remember that moment with the kind of feeling you get on the downside of a roller-coaster ride. By the time I left that meeting in Knoxville I knew it was all over for me as the new senator from Tennessee.

But running at the 48 percent level gave me the name recognition, the credibility, the element of surprise that propelled me into the Senate race in 1966. I never really stopped running those next two years and the victory was worth it.

Future historians are going to look at the late twentieth century from a much different perspective than we do as we play out the events of our own lives. They will discern rhythms and meanings that we can see obscurely at best, as we put together the small stones of action that actually become the edifice of history.

It's one of our cherished premises that ancient Athens was one of the principal seeding grounds of modern Western democracy. But we can be pretty sure that the men who drove off the hordes of the Persian Empire were concerned only with the preservation of their own lives and the sustenance of their own values. History is always for the future. Although each of us has a part in making the record that writers and scholars can ponder tomorrow, our real job is to make a success of *now*.

It's our job to lead productive individual lives as members of a human society of staggering complexity at the same time as we forge ties with each other that are strong, stable, and mutually satisfactory. If we do that, history will take care of itself.

We hear much talk about malaise and decline and uncertainty. It's natural enough to feel some discomfort after going through the roller coaster of depression, world war, cold war, Korea, Vietnam, Watergate, and the worst economic crisis since the 1930's. But the simple fact is that the American people didn't produce a cornucopia of wealth and well-being and generosity out of feelings of self-pity. And if we're to restore those satisfactions we need hard work and high spirits.

The Chinese say that it's not a nice thing to wish that someone's children live in interesting times. Well, we do live in interesting times. So do our children, and all of us better make the most of it. This is the time to take the steps that restore a communal purpose and a sense of direction to individual lives. The best way to do that is to analyze how and why we find ourselves on the unfamiliar terrain of national uncertainty and dissatisfaction.

How did we get here? Where do we want to be? What do we have to do to get there?

For nearly three hundred years North America has been a testing ground for human resourcefulness and social cohesion. The men and women who first settled on the eastern forest fringes were followed by tens of millions more who moved slowly but inexorably across the three thousand miles that then separated and now link the Atlantic and Pacific oceans. It was a march of settlement that was sometimes a crawl and frequently a series of battles for survival or plunder or both. It brought into being a continental nation of staggering resources in wealth, and a variety of people beyond the imaginations of those first pilgrims who ventured hesitantly on a voyage that is still far from over.

We have good reason to be an optimistic people. In two hundred years of national history there's been more than enough difficulty to keep everyone busy. Wars, depression, racial division, and bloody civil conflict have pockmarked this country's existence. But we have almost always had a sense that as a society we would handle any problem that came down the pike. Some of the solutions proposed to our political and social dilemmas by the factions that inevitably develop in a huge and turbulent and changing and filling country were less than polite. Some were downright stupid, some were venal, some were actually vicious; still, far more often than not, the American system had produced out of its structured and tumultuous diversity the kind of answers to the practical problems of getting along together that have made it possible for individuals to concentrate on advancing the well-being of their families and themselves. For most of our history we have looked to a democratic government to do just that. But a new orthodoxy of elitism threatens to change the fundamental nature of self-government as we have known it. Personal decisions about the way we live our everyday lives are increasingly made under the constraints of anonymous rulemakers. I call them the irresponsible governors.

Process is the method by which any business is done, including the business of government, and the Constitution's very elasticity has sustained its life as our supreme instrument of government. Yet that same rubber-band quality accounts in large part for the growth of an extra-constitutional jungle of statute and regulation that threatens in 1980 to choke off sustained and healthy national growth.

Some recent developments even raise questions about our ability to deal effectively with the political and social issues we must meet.

More and more Americans have become angered and bewildered at the Washington mandarins who decide on everything from how many potatoes a farmer may pack in a box to whether or not Congress passed a law to forbid having a father and son dinner in your local high school.

Joe Califano, the former secretary of Health, Education, and Welfare, is a good friend of mine. We almost never agree about public issues because Joe is the unapologetic essence of Johnsonian bureaucracy. He believes in big government, big programs, and he believes in tough administration of them. I never will forget the first time I saw him in that great big, cavernous, ornate office of the secretary of Health, Education, and Welfare. It was in the midst of an antismoking campaign that Joe had started, and there he was, puffing like a chimney stack. "Do as I say, not as I do" is one of the unwritten principles of big government.

It is a bitter paradox that this new orthodoxy of close federal supervision of local government, as well as individual and family life, is the natural outgrowth of a successful attempt to find solutions to an earlier set of problems. But we're active participants in a case of the cure threatening to kill the patient, and the patient is us!

In the early 1930's and 1940's the United States responded with skilled determination to the challenge of worldwide depression and war. Congress granted unparalleled emergency power to the President, and the use to which that power was put created a new set of social and political expectations among most of our people.

Government was coming to be seen as the beneficent source of the good things of life by citizens who formerly regarded it as an agency to offer police and fire protection, ward off foreign enemies, and act as referee in the sometimes savage economic and social disputes that inevitably arise in tens of thousands of private arenas. In the desperate battle for economic survival and in the crucible of war, disparate and frequently antagonistic groups and interests submerged their differences. With government as both leader and arbiter they forged a unity that raised the United States to economic and military power unparalleled in world history.

It was a heady time. The country was embarked on a binge of apparently unending growth, unending government intervention in the marketplace, unending government regulation of private decision-making, and unending government failure to respond to the real world. But the signs that the bill would have to be paid slowly began to appear.

In 1950 the civilian payroll of the United States was less than $8 billion. In 1968 that payroll had grown to $58 billion. Meanwhile, the American productivity that had produced 50,000 airplanes a year when we needed them to fight World War II had declined in real terms from an annual growth rate of 2.6 percent in 1967 to less than 1 percent in 1977 and the years that follow. At the same time as the 1967 dollar plunged to fifty-two cents in 1979, American productivity ranked dead last among the leading ten nations of the West.

The terrifying inflation combined with economic recession that today threatens our political and economic foundations is a direct outgrowth of the refusal to change policies conceived and originally implemented to solve the problems of another time. The excessive government that threatens to smother us is unnatural to a free society and by definition it is unresponsive both to the will of the people and the people's elected representatives. The low productivity that stagnates the strength of our commerce results from high taxation. And the American people are close to being taxed to death in order to redistribute a shrinking economic pie. Yet with all the issues we confront, we do live in a good society that is well worth preserving from poor policy at home and hostile threats from abroad.

There are reasonable ways to respond to differences among fellow members of the international community in a fashion that will satisfy both justice and equity. But going on a guilt trip because we are a fortunate people, because our awesome power has infrequently been badly used, is a perverse starting point for the determination and execution of foreign policy. There isn't a nation in the world that can claim a record of international generosity equal to ours. If there are scales of international justice, the United States weighs well in the balance.

The most important thing to remember in the 1980's is that we must make difficult choices in a real world that is not always hospitable to our values, sometimes envious of our wealth, and fearful of the consequences of our power.

Some politicians and analysts wince at the word "linkage." It has become an "issue" word like "détente." But linkage is a recognition of the simple fact that the political world reflects a universe in which every action is linked in one way or another, and every cause has countless effects.

In the real world, foreign and domestic policies are closely related, and the way we govern ourselves determines their direction. That's why it's time to make a new beginning in the way the United States government deals with the problems of its own people at home, and the growing instability of the larger world in which we must live and survive.

In the following pages I intend to examine in some detail the nature of the problems we face and some of the ways in which we may begin to find their solutions. I hope that you will come to share with me the belief that many seemingly intractable issues will yield to a determined and unified effort to resolve them even at the cost of abandoning yesterday's dogmas. We must analyze our situation, decide what we must do, and act on our decisions.

2

The Founding Fathers, the *Federal Register*, and "Staying Home from Politics"

In 1970 there were 203 million people living in the United States. If the experts are right, there will be 20 million more when the results of the 1980 census are in. That's almost a quarter of a billion people living in a prosperous and self-governing republic. It's a staggering conception when you think that there were only 4 million Americans when George Washington took the oath of office as the country's first President. After 150 years of European settlement and struggle, the United States was still a strip of sparsely settled farms and cities along the eastern seaboard of a largely unexplored and threatening continent. But a political miracle of sorts had already occurred (and we've had plenty since).

Four million people, still fairly clinging to the edges of the new world, created a climate in which its citizenry weighed, accepted, and gave life to the Constitution of the United States.

The few hundred political leaders of the thirteen colonies who actually determined the direction of the new republic, and the few dozen who wrote the declaration of its independence and its governing document, were almost unique in human history. Scholars tell us that the richness of their intellects, the quality of their vision, and the restraints they placed on their individual self-interest hadn't been equaled since democracy took its first steps in ancient Athens. But their most remarkable accomplishment was not the nobility of their expression or even the quality of the government they instituted among themselves. The most important political act of that or any generation before or since was their creation of a nuts-and-bolts blueprint for government that has survived as a working document for 191 years.

The Constitution is so often invoked as a kind of semi-religious object that we forget the miracle of what it really is. The men who wrote that Constitution for a small and homogeneous population (all rooted in Western Europe, and most from the British Isles), on a continent comfortably distant from much of the turmoil of their ancestral homes, made a document that still serves as an umbrella of governing principles for the world's most rapidly changing and growing civilization.

These were men who couldn't know about the internal combustion machine, or the power of the atom, or the civil and global wars to come, or the flooding of a thriving empire with immigrants from eastern and southern Europe and Africa and Asia and Central and South America. They had no knowledge of the automobiles and the airplanes and the great railroads that were to forge a continental republic from the thirteen colonies in which they lived.

Somehow, without that knowledge, with no record that implies anything but the vaguest prescience of what was to come, they made a set of governing principles that are central to the life of twentieth-century Americans. If anything, the Constitution has a significance to citizens living today that goes far beyond the impact any political covenant could have had on the rural people who first lived under its rubric.

From the beginning, the Constitution has been read by different eyes in many different ways. Its most enduring quality is the opportunity it has given succeeding generations to interpret it in accord with the needs of their own times.

Perhaps the secret is that the Constitution is a short document. There are only 7,500 words, and that includes all twenty-six amendments that have been adopted since 1789. Any young lawyer worth his or her degree can write a brief on one constitutional clause that's longer than the entire text. A number of policy-makers have come to feel that a document subject to such detailed exegesis and differences of interpretation needs a stringent overhauling. But I believe that we have a more than serviceable document for our own time; and we certainly have had enough practice in amending it when that has been necessary to accommodate to new attitudes and the changing will of the people.

That is the central strength in the Constitution. It has, historically, been adapted to the will of the people; not the *whim*, but the overwhelming *will*, as articulated in the detailed and frequently emotional dialogue that always precedes the passage of a constitutional amendment. We may not all agree as to whether one or the other of the amendments that is now part of the Constitution should have been adopted. But only the willfully blind would contend that those amendments have failed to reflect the strong beliefs of the majority of the political constituency.

The Constitution has thus provided a frame for democratic government in keeping with an egalitarianism that grew with American expansion in territory, power, and a surging and heterogeneous population. In 1980 it is hard to remember that a distinguished American historian, Charles Beard, once wrote a major work that analyzed the Constitution as a document produced by a small oligarchy of landowners determined to protect their own economic interests against the mob!

But if the Constitution is a document to satisfy all of the social orders that have been implanted in America, it offers no easy answers to the problems that inevitably arise in the day-to-day business of government.

It would have been beyond the most nightmarish visions

of any of the founding fathers that in 1980 there would be any such thing as the *Federal Register*.

You should know about the *Federal Register* because it influences almost every aspect of your life. Each and every year the *Federal Register* publishes 60,000 legally binding regulations. It might just as well be called "your guide to everyday living" because it publishes rules that have to do with the coffee you drink, the toothpaste you choose, how much interest your bank can pay you, as well as where and how your children go to school.

The rules promulgated in the *Federal Register* are not laws passed by Congress. But they have every bit of the force of law and too frequently they use the law as a pretext to impose the beliefs of civil servants who may sometimes disagree with the intent of the law as written.

The *Federal Register* has become a kind of daily addition to the Constitution of the United States. It is the surface expression of much of the work done by the executive branch of the government and the regulatory agencies (most of them are ostensibly independent) that grind out millions of pages of paper work for ordinary citizens to do. As a matter of fact, the President of the United States recently thought it necessary to appoint still another commission. This one is supposed to study whether or not there's a way to reduce the federal paper logjam. So far the commission has succeeded only in adding more pulp to the already choking stream. No wonder the shortage of newsprint threatens to drive a good many smaller newspapers out of business.

But the important question is whether or not the staggering range of subject and content in the *Register* is an incursion of bureaucratic power that is at odds with the spirit of the Constitution and with the fundamental principles of self-government.

In 1936, the first year of the *Federal Register*'s regular publication, some 2,619 pages of bureaucratic rulemaking were printed. Let's not forget that in 1936 the United States was in the trough of the Great Depression. For the first time in American history the federal government was involved in massive across-the-board intervention in American life. Once that kind of intervention begins, the law of inertia takes over. By 1970 the *Federal Register* was publishing over 20,000 pages annually. In 1976, 57,000 pages of federal regulation were bound in the *Federal Register*. And in 1980—only four years later—it is estimated that 100,000 pages of *Federal Register* material will have been published since the year began. The level of the paper machine's output is hardly the most significant measure of government interference in the minutiae of our everyday lives. But it is certainly a symbolic expression of the aggravation to which we have become accustomed. Brood with me on this IRS regulation as embodied in one of those 100,000 pages put out in 1980:

> Bread crumbs treated so as to simulate salmon eggs and pork rind, cut and dyed to resemble frogs, eels, or tadpoles are considered to be "artificial fishing lures."

That means, under IRS rules, that these particular bread crumbs are subject to an excise tax. But, ever alert, the IRS took great care to evaluate a fishing bait made of chicken blood that's processed into patties. It is, according to the *Federal Register*, "still identifiable as chicken blood." Inasmuch as it hasn't been made to "resemble another article more attractive to fish," the bait is exempt from the tax.

Thus the *Federal Register*! Who's baiting whom?

According to the text of a workbook issued by the people who give you the *Federal Register*, "Congress delegates the authority to agencies to implement the law of Congress. In this respect *regulations can be considered delegated legislation*." Inasmuch as Congress cannot constitutionally delegate its legislative authority, such an observation is peculiarly revealing of a bureaucratic mind set at odds with the principles of self-government. But it would be most unfair to lay the blame for that mind set on the men and women who operate the bureaucracy. The sad fact is that Congress has, to all intents and purposes, abdicated a substantial portion of its obligation to make the substantive law of the United States. Vacuums in authority are apparently subject to the laws of physics. No matter how, they will be filled. But it does raise a serious question as to what has happened to our representative democracy.

The growth of regulation has had another, wholly unexpected effect. The federal court system has intruded itself into the day-to-day business of government.

In this generation we have seen a change in the way the courts view their roles and a reluctance on the part of Congress to draw the line. It is no great feat of the imagination to see a constitutional crisis down the road.

I remember a story about the Supreme Court that made the rounds when I was in law school. It seems a young lawyer who was arguing his first case was going on about some proposition when the Chief Justice interrupted him and said, "Young man, that's not the law." The young fellow said, "Well, it was the law until Your Honor spoke." That tale illustrates the absolute power of the Supreme Court in judicial matters. Whatever they interpret the law to be, it is the law. That lends itself, then, to the law being different things at different times.

Baker v. *Carr* is a good example of the process. The Supreme Court had consistently held that reapportionment and redistricting were political matters and could not be intruded on by the federal government. Then the Warren Court, in *Baker* v. *Carr,* held that it was an infringement of equal protection of the laws to hold elections that give more electoral weight to a vote in one part of a state than another. From that day on the law meant something totally new. That may or may not have been implicit in the first decisions that created the authority of the Court to review legislative and executive action. But it has become a part of constitutional tradition and it means in effect that the Court can act in a quasi-legislative manner.

The Warren Court was the most activist in recent years, certainly in civil rights and social policy. I knew Earl Warren over a period of time. He seemed to be a very unlikely personality to lead such an activist Court. He was jovial and almost jolly. He gave the impression of avoiding controversy rather than mediating it. On the bench he was courtly. I remember when Estes Kefauver and my father stood by me as I was introduced to the Supreme Court that Warren made almost a social occasion out of it.

If you read his decisions you'll find that they were complex, sometimes wandered, almost never were they scholarly, but they were extraordinary. They plowed new ground.

I had the same impression of Earl Warren as I have of almost every other Supreme Court member. They're hungry for companionship. They feel removed, or at least insulated, from the political process. Every time I see one of them I get the impression that they long for social chatter. They like to hear the little stories and I'm always tempted to ask them over for lunch. They should show themselves and get out into the world. I think it was a mistake that we let them move out of the Capitol, where they held court for many, many years. It would be good for them if they did come up and have lunch. It would have a great humanizing effect.

I know Potter Stewart as well as any of the justices. We got acquainted when he was on the Sixth Circuit Court of Appeals. I argued a few cases before him and won some, lost some. He's what I call a Cincinnati lawyer.

Cincinnati lawyers are a special breed. They're gentlemanly, midwestern, nonpontifical, and very, very skillful. Potter is in that mold, although I disagree with some of his judicial views as expressed in court decisions.

The abortion issue was, I believe, the least appropriate

of subjects for the Supreme Court's consideration. It is so sensitive an issue, and so peculiar to the social mores of particular areas and beliefs, that, at the very most, the states should establish the guidelines for abortion. Since the Court opened the question to federal guidance that view is no longer viable because Congress is continually involved with that thorny problem of federal funds for abortion.

The most obvious and widely noted intrusion of the courts into government administration is closely linked to school busing. When school districts have not conformed to court-dictated administrative remedies with sufficient alacrity, courts have simply taken over the schools. That means the judges run them without reference to the wishes of the people and their elected representatives. It is a practice that has produced the symptoms of increased racial tension at a time when there is every reason for it to disappear.

But the school-busing situation is only the tip of the iceberg of the increasing practice of government by judge.

The courts have also taken it on themselves to assume jurisdiction over prisons, hospitals, and other institutions whenever the practices or the standards of the authorities in charge have failed to meet some arbitrarily and subjectively determined constitutional precept. There has been much anger but little legislative response to this new judicial activism. But, in my view, government by judiciary is diametrically opposed to the principles of the separation of powers. It is only a matter of time before justified limits are placed on the practice of judicial interference. When and if the battle comes it will be a contest of enormous significance because we, as a people, have historically deferred to the judicial power as an instrument of arbitration. It is for the future to decide whether we can continue to do so if it breaks the spirit of the Constitution it must uphold. I'm convinced of one thing. Judges, as a rule, are too far removed from the give-and-take of everyday life to make good executives and legislators, even if they had the *right* to do those jobs.

I've given considerable thought to the Court and its role. I had to because I almost became a Supreme Court justice myself. Bill Rehnquist has the seat that I might have had. When John Mitchell was attorney general he called me one day and I went down to see him at the Justice Department. I'd known John as a lawyer for some time, long before he got into government. He asked what I would do if President Nixon offered me a seat on the Supreme Court, and I said, "I think I wish he wouldn't do that." He asked why. I told him that it would pose a real dilemma for me because I enjoyed what I was doing. Mitchell asked me to think about it. After that, I went over to see Potter Stewart. That was the first and only time I've ever been in the Court's private chambers. I talked to Potter about what their life was like, what they did when the Court wasn't in session, and how many clerks they had. I looked around, and talked with him about the Court's life. It reminded me so much of law school, and I never was really fond of law school, that I had to say my appetite was not whetted. Finally, I told Mitchell that if the President insisted that I do it I would feel I must, but I really would prefer to stay where I was. He said, "Since you feel that way, I think we'd all be better off if we went with Rehnquist."

I never for a moment regretted that decision not to accept a seat on the Court, because for me the heart of representative government is elective politics.

Yet, we have to ask whether free elections alone provide adequate assurance that the American people are running their own country. I think a pretty good case can be made that free election is only a step toward self-government and that many Americans feel excluded from the decisions that affect the quality of their lives.

Only 36 percent of eligible voters went to the polls on

election day in 1978. Compare that with the figures in other places where people are allowed to make up their own minds as to whether or not they vote. In England, 70 percent recently chose the people who are going to lead them. In France it's 80 percent; in Austria it's 90 percent. Even in Italy, where government is generally thought to be at a standstill most of the time, 85 percent of the voters go to the polls at every election. In Japan, a country which has had a democratic government only since 1945, the number is 68 percent, and in West Germany it's 85 percent.

That suggests a profound alienation or indifference on the part of a majority of Americans to the processes of the very government that affects their lives more and more as each day passes.

The numbers send us an even more distressing signal. The younger the prospective voter, the less likely he or she is to show up at the polls on election day; this in a country that passed a constitutional amendment to permit eighteen-year-olds to vote.

The theme of the campaign for the eighteen-year-old vote, for those readers too young to remember, was "If you're old enough to fight for your country, you're old enough to vote for its leaders." Fair enough. But where are the beneficiaries of the amendment? Why don't they come out?

I think I understand in my bones the reason the indifferents stay at home. They don't think *they* count. They don't believe that who they vote for, what party they vote for, will mean a solitary thing to them in their individual lives.

There's a real paradox at work in party politics right now. The old city machines are well on the way out; and good riddance. I remember the way old Ed Crump had a lock on Shelby County and the city of Memphis for almost too many years to count.

He ran a good city, he ran a clean city, he ran an efficient organization. As far as I could tell in the daily affairs of the city, its fiscal affairs, it was an honest city. But it was corrupt politics. It was just the kind of politics that turns people off. I recall when my father ran for governor in 1938. He was a young man, thirty-seven years old. He got 1,179 votes in Shelby County at the same time as his running mate for the U.S. Senate received only 100 votes fewer in that same county. That was clearly impossible. There'd be more *mistakes* than that in a total vote of 200,000 or whatever Shelby County had at the time.

They tell a great story about the bivalence of Mr. Crump's honesty in administration and his shady political operations. Mr. Crump and his close associate Will Gerber walked into the graveyard one night taking names to vote the dead people on the tombstones the next day. And they were writing them down and writing them down, and it was sort of dark and dim, and they came to one tombstone and Will held up the flashlight and rubbed against the name and the date and couldn't quite make it out, and Gerber said, "Mr. Ed, I can't quite make this one out. Shall we just put down another name?" Crump said, "No, Will, you gotta remember we run a clean election."

Most of the Crump people weren't venal. But it was such an authoritarian politics that I simply cannot believe that it had any redeeming grace whatever. Even though the machine was too high a price to pay for orderliness, we have to recognize that a different and legitimate party structure has to replace it if voters are going to feel that they have a stake in the system, that the parties are genuinely responsive to people.

What we need at this point in history are strong, highly effective, well-organized state political organizations and the changing presidential nominating system is beginning to accomplish just that. The only purpose and justification that a political party has in the American scheme is to compete for the opportunity to represent the multiple interests and views of a majority of the people. The party's philosophy will evolve based on its membership and its points of view at a particular time and place. This kind of political apparatus must be strengthened by much closer contact with the grassroots. It should be armed with the full array of patronage opportunities, of the power of appointment, of protection of citizens from a predatory government. And it should encourage a political President who understands that politics is a legitimate and sustaining enterprise.

Something dangerous has happened when mainstream Americans have decided to stay home from politics. A kind of disease has spread through the system and it's time that we cure it. It's a disease that first manifested itself among the American blacks and Hispanics who were forced by circumstance to live on the economic and social margins of society. As these groups move into the social and economic action they increasingly need to participate in the political process. But even as late as 1978 too many blacks and Puerto Ricans and Chicanos missed the opportunity to make themselves felt at the polls. Only 37 percent of the black voters participated in the congressional elections of 1978, and 23.5 percent of the Hispanic population voted. That's an improvement over past performance, but it tells us that, like increasing numbers of younger people and older Americans who have broken the voting habit, there is a tendency to regard politics as a futile game for someone else to play.

Let's do something about it. Let's register voters automatically so that every American can vote in federal elections at age eighteen. The history of the United States has been a history of the extension of the voting franchise. Yet, even today, a significant number of our people are effectively prevented from participating in elections by complex, and often archaic, registration and residency requirements.

Several Western nations have already successfully implemented a form of automatic voter registration. In the Scandinavian countries and in Switzerland every eligible citizen is registered *ex officio* in a voting register. A list of voters is published by the elections authorities in advance of the election date. Any citizen whose name has not been included in the list then has until approximately a week before the election to correct the situation. In the United States, however, citizens still must contend with what amounts to a perpetual registration process. Serious difficulties would doubtless crop up in translating automatic registration to the realities of the American experience and attempting to reconcile it with state registration procedures. Social Security numbers might be utilized to standardize the procedure. More than 95 percent of eligible voters are already registered with Social Security. We ought to consider any device that will encourage an end to stay-at-home politicking.

We must also add still more genuine significance to the presidential primaries. One possibility would require all the primary states to hold them on four or five specific dates at two- or three-week intervals. Other alternatives might be a single national primary for each party with a subsequent runoff unless one candidate polls more than 40 percent, or a system of regional primaries also held at specific intervals, but encompassing all of the country.

I'm inclined to support a system of regional primaries in which every eligible voter who desires to participate in the selection of a party nominee can do so by voting in the regional primary that includes his state. This would permit the millions of Americans who support candidates who will not receive the party nomination to express that support in a meaningful way. It would also give them a personal stake in the election and increase the likelihood of their participation in the subsequent general election campaign.

Specifically, I would propose dividing the country into four geographic regions, largely along the lines of time zones so as to avoid holding a "southern" or a "New England" primary with a distinct ideological slant. I would make those regions of roughly equal population and would hold the four primaries at three-week intervals beginning in early June and ending in early August. Each would compete for state delegates who would be won according to the proportion of vote received in each state rather than on a winner-take-all basis. Although I am aware of the high cost involved in running in regional primaries, the basic idea is to vastly expand the public participation in the nominating process and to *significantly reduce the official length of presidential campaigns.*

As it is now, the first presidential primary or caucus takes place in late January, with the general election ten months later in November. But, as I see it, there is absolutely no reason why that process must take that long. It costs exorbitant sums of money, and bores a great many people. I think that eventually all primaries for federal office should be held no earlier than the first of June and no later than the fifteenth of August. This would significantly shorten the official length of campaigns for federal office and permit the Congress to work at relatively full strength for four months before most members are forced to return to their states or districts to campaign full time for the nomination.

We should also open and close polls all across the country at a uniform time and keep them open a full twenty-four hours. That's the best way I know of to prevent the harmful effects of broadcast networks projecting the outcome of elections, based on very early returns, when polls in the western states are still open. Moreover, twenty-four hours would maximize the individual's opportunity to vote before, after, or during work.

The presidential electoral system should also be made more responsive and representative by the abolition of the electoral college, an eighteenth-century vestigial remnant of constitutional compromise. I favor and have always supported the direct election of the President by popular vote, but having unsuccessfully urged that move, I am willing to settle for an improvement if not a cure for this situation. Congress and the states should fully debate the merits of

popular vote, congressional district vote, proportional allocation of electoral votes by states according to the popular vote,
or any other electoral process calculated to eliminate what I
view as the two undemocratic elements of the present system.
The first is the winner-take-all process, which created and
perpetuated the one-party South for a century after the
Civil War; and the second is the possibility of the selection
of the President by the House of Representatives. That is
simply no way to elect a President in a democracy. The
sensitivity of the electoral system, the coherence of the selection process, and the vitality of the two-party system are essential to the political prosperity of the country and are paramount in their importance to every other consideration.

But no mechanism we can devise will combat that part of
what the pollsters call "voter apathy" that is an outgrowth
of about thirty years of increasingly arbitrary and unresponsive government action.

Anonymous government officials issue confusing and frequently conflicting instructions on a daily and sometimes
hourly basis. They can range in importance from the likely
direction of radioactive fallout in a nuclear accident to the
mandatory size and shape of a safety helmet that must be
worn by California motorcyclists under the threat of a federal cutoff of that state's highway safety funds.

Potomac Survey and Lou Harris and Dan Yankelovich
and George Gallup and dozens of others who specialize in
one aspect or another of public opinion and behavior have
all come to the conclusion that there is significantly less confidence in the President and in Congress than ever before.
If an individual member of Congress thought that his constituents felt he was as ineffectual as they feel about Congress
as a whole, he would be tempted to throw up the job and go
home. But the fact is that people don't blame individual
members of Congress; they blame the institution itself for
being inadequate to the job it is elected to do. President
Carter, who has taken the most dramatic roller-coaster ride

in the history of public-opinion polling, is also increasingly regarded as a good man in the wrong job. Some of the polls that probe more deeply into why people think and feel the way they do indicate that there is a more than casual belief that the fulfillment of the presidency is now beyond the capacity of anyone in a way that will give positive direction to the country's economic and social life. I disagree. Our institutions are viable in themselves, as they have been for two hundred years. The trouble is that they have been misused and abused.

Political scientists and specialists in government don't take into sufficient account the play of human passion that infuses the process with life. When I hear discussions about the significance of what happened at a particular hearing or the "meaning" of the way a debate was handled on the Senate floor I sometimes shake my head in wonderment. It's like reading about a game between the Washington Redskins and the Dallas Cowboys as though it were played by those little X's and O's that coaches like to put on their blackboards. Who would want to watch anything like that on a Sunday afternoon? Big men are hitting each other hard and that's what the yelling is all about. In those pile-ups on the field some pretty violent things happen and that, unfortunately, is a piece of what life is all about. Constitutions and statutes provide a framework for human action. But the emphasis is on the word "human."

Bob Byrd is the most skillful Senate parliamentarian I have seen, by far. He has made a study of the rules and precedents of the Senate that I hope someday he will record for the legislators of the future. He is as close to being a true creature of the procedural Senate as any man could be. He has a second skill that is less often observed, and that is to weld together that disparate group on the Democratic side of the Senate. In a lot of ways he has a tougher job than I do in trying to keep the Republicans together simply because there are more of them, and they probably do have a broader spectrum of differences of view on their side. He does it very well. It takes a lot of bending and twisting sometimes, and I frequently suspect that Bob Byrd has to abdicate some points of view that he holds himself in order to accomplish his leadership goals. That's sometimes a necessary part of the process. Byrd incurs a lot of enmity, on both sides of the aisle, as a hard driver; that is, he has no compunction about running the Senate late and bringing it in early. He's fiercely partisan, a quality I am certainly not one to criticize. Each of us was elected to lead our parties in the Senate, and though we frequently differ on issues, we cooperate to keep the Senate moving.

I meet with ranking Republican members of all Senate committees at least once a week to try to get a fix on what's coming up for decision. Byrd and I trade visits several times every day to deal with the legislative calendar. An interesting aspect of Senate life is the custom that requires the majority and minority leaders to work out *mutually* satisfactory arrangements as to what, how, and when the Senate will consider a bill or a presidential appointment. If comity breaks down the Senate will grind to a halt. That's how Black Monday came about in October of 1978.

It all started when the Senate found itself tied up in a wrangle over whether or not to deregulate natural gas prices. The votes were there to do it, but a minority of senators, led by Howard Metzenbaum of Ohio and Jim Abourezk of South Dakota, refused to let it come to a vote. They led a filibuster by amendment. Abourezk, a Senate maverick who had a reputation for going his own way, offered hundreds of amendments to the bipartisan Pearson–Bentsen bill designed to phase out regulation that inhibited additional fuel production. The Senate stayed in session eighteen to twenty hours a day in an attempt to break the filibuster. Cots were brought into my office, to the caucus room, and to the cloakrooms. The lights burned all night long. But the two senators were in great physical condition and stood their ground on the right, hallowed by long custom, to offer and debate amendment after amendment.

Finally, on Sunday afternoon, Bob Byrd and I met in the majority leader's office, just a few feet off the Senate chamber, to see if we could settle this thing. Bill Hildenbrand, the Senate minority secretary, is in many ways my strong right arm. He was with me. Scoop Jackson, Russell Long, and Murray Zweben, the Senate parliamentarian, also participated.

The difficulty was that people always find different ways to get around the anti-filibuster rule. Jim Allen, the late senator from Alabama, was a past master at using the intricacies of the Senate rules to delay debate. Metzenbaum and Abourezk used a variation on the Jim Allen theorem, and that is filibuster by amendment. They put in four or five hundred amendments, and even if there were no time for debate, the rules permitted them to have the amendments voted on. So they'd call up an amendment; somebody would suggest the absence of a quorum, which is a constitutional right and can't be abrogated; the chair would read the amendment, which might be hundreds of pages long; then there was a quorum call. It would take thirty minutes or an hour to assemble a quorum. You could go on for months like that. They had perfected a new filibuster art form and Byrd became more and more incensed. It was clear that we weren't going to be able to break this thing unless we plowed some new ground at our meeting.

Byrd wanted to propose some rules changes. But I wouldn't do that because the minority party can be seriously damaged once we begin changing the rules to accommodate to a particular circumstance. Byrd knew that he couldn't steamroll us, that we could hold all the Republicans together on something like changes in the rules. So we began exploring other possibilities. We agreed on the objective: that we had to get this thing shut down and pass that bill. In the course of the conversation Byrd or the parliamentarian pointed out that Rule 22 prohibits dilatory motions. Why not establish a precedent that if you had already had a quorum call since the last vote, then another such call was dilatory? The premise was that if you've got five hundred amendments, you know full well they're dilatory. The sticky question was what to do about the right of any senator to appeal the ruling of the chair. That was the toughest decision for me to make because it was an exercise in raw power.

One of the few real powers that a majority or a minority leader has is for preferential recognition. If there are twenty people standing up or eighty people standing up seeking recognition, the chair by precedent must recognize the majority leader first and then the minority leader. That's a powerful legislative weapon. We decided that Byrd and I would use the power of prior recognition to prevent further filibustering. He'd call up one amendment after the other and get it ruled out of order. We went through hundreds of amendments that way, with everybody screaming, beating on the desks, and carrying on. That's the only time in my career I've ever used pure raw power.

But I first said, "Look, if we're going to do this deed, if we're going to do these things, boys, you have that Vice-President in the chair. The White House is going to share the responsibility for this."

On Monday at noon Fritz Mondale took the chair. The majority leader and I stood at our aisle desks. The Vice President recognized me so that I could make a point of order that would set the stage for what followed. I said that it was my view that an amendment that had been offered, and ruled out of order, was no longer pending business before the Senate. That meant that a quorum call was not in order either. The filibustering Senators were thus deprived of their principal delaying tactic. Mondale accepted the point and Byrd addressed him in one of the Senate's most dramatic moments.

"Mr. President, I call up unprinted Metzenbaum Amendment Number Forty-two to Calendar Item Number Sixty-seven." Mondale replied, "The amendment is dilatory and out of order." "Mr. President, I call up unprinted Abourezk Amendment Number Forty-three . . ." Again Mondale repeated, "The amendment is dilatory and out of order," Byrd and I looked straight ahead, ignoring the murmur of disapproval that began to swell around us. We called up amendment after amendment. There were shouts for recognition from around the chamber, but the Vice-President kept his eyes riveted on Byrd and Baker. He wasn't about to recognize anyone on a point of order or for anything else until he had ruled almost all of the filibuster amendments out of order. I have never heard the chamber in such disorder as on that Black Monday.

When the last amendment had been ruled out of order, the Vice-President recognized an angered and shaken Javits of New York. Javits spoke for the majority of the senators when he told the chair that the Senate rules had been bent if not broken, and that it was a classic case of using the ends to justify the means.

Senators call that day Black Monday because we can never be sure of what it bodes for the future. The rules are designed to keep things moving. But both the rules and custom provide a strong bulwark against tyranny of the majority. Every time we bend those rules out of shape, every time we break custom rooted in time, we walk along a dangerous precipice.

What we did was perfectly legal. We didn't change any rules and we didn't prejudice any Republican rights; but we really did treat the filibuster senators shabbily because we flat cut them out with the power of the leadership. I sympathized with the Javits position, but it had to be done.

Too many people in positions of influence and power have passed a kind of Parkinson's law that more red tape is better red tape. They insist that excessive legislation, over-regulation, and constant executive tampering with the minutiae of everyday life is the kind of government that we must have to satisfy our economic and social needs. That kind of government failed us in the 1970's. We will insist in the 1980's on a government that sees to it that the United States maintains the military and the economic strength necessary to survive as a democracy (a government that sharply revises federal statutes that interfere with individual liberties at the expense of economic stability, growth, and productivity) and a government that hacks away at the accretion of tens of thousands of regulations that choke our enterprise.

We have the materials at hand to build the kind of country most Americans want to live in at the end of the 1980's. What kind of country can it be?

3

Productivity, Snail Darters and Leaky Rowboats

American productivity has been the key to the staggering economic power exercised by our industrial and commercial enterprise here at home and throughout the world. At the end of the 1970's it became obvious that this linchpin of the American success had worn out. No rational observer can fail to link the weakening of productivity with the almost unbelievable reduction in the dollar's buying power.

From 1965 to 1973 American manufacturing companies produced everything from widgets to golf clubs, from automobiles to aircrafts in a quantity and quality that made it possible for us to achieve an unparalleled standard of living. Economic growth has historically been reflected in every kind of statistical analysis made of this country's development. Whether the focus is on the gross national product or the rise in individual income, or the level of savings, or any one of the indices that experts formulate, Americans had a reason to be confident in the future. But in the last five years the numbers changed, the confidence waned, and puzzlement swept through the academic community that had made the measurements in the first place. Their puzzlement quickly spread to people in every walk of life and in every place in the country. I remember talking with a friend in

Knoxville shortly after he was forced to close a business that had employed 350 skilled workers. "Howard," he said, "I feel like I've been run over by a runaway horse. I just don't know what happened. We've been doing the same things in the same way for fifteen years. One day we're making money, and the next day we're closing the door. How can doing the right thing turn into doing the wrong thing so quick?"

That question has been asked over and over again by businessmen, politicians, labor leaders, and the American housewife, who spends more and more of her supermarket money for less and less in the grocery bag. The fact is that the American economy is in a tailspin because government has scrambled up its priorities for action, and an inflated dollar is by definition a weak dollar. There is now more money worth less, producing fewer goods. And some will tell you that *they're* worth less, too.

One of our problems in solving this sudden multicrisis of values is the dramatic suddenness of its appearance. Once we get a handle on what's happening and why, we can do something about it. Inflation and declining productivity are the inevitable outgrowths of government spending that has become totally unrelated to government resources. Every dollar that the U.S. takes from your pocket in taxation, every dollar that the U.S. government spends on an entitlement program is a dollar that is unavailable for investment in the productive part of the economy. We have to remember, you and I, that government doesn't produce a single solid thing. But we've reached a point in which government takes twenty-two cents out of every dollar that we earn and says without a thank you or a by-your-leave that this is what we're going to do with that twenty-two cents. And as inflation increases so does government's share of the gross national product. Economists say that at the current rate of spending the federal government will suck in for its own purposes 24 percent of GNP by 1983. That means almost one out of every four dollars you earn is taken out of the country's mainstream.

At this rate the American people are going to run out of more than one kind of fuel. For stable currency is required to build the economic plant that sustains us today while it builds the foundation for a larger and more complicated world tomorrow. When that *real money* fuel runs short, the federal government has got itself into the nasty habit of continuing to spend. If Howard Baker did that, or if any of you did that, our checks would bounce with a snap that would be hurtful to both our reputations and our credit. But that is not the way it has worked for the men and women who decide on the federal budget. When they don't have the wherewithal to pay for a new boondoggle, or to pay for a worthwhile program (and there are many of those —it's a complicated world and there are choices we have to make), they simply print more money. That's called deficit spending and only the federal government can get away with it without paying the piper. That simply means that the federal government won't go to jail. But there is a subtle irony here because that protection enjoyed by Uncle Sam is largely illusory.

As those deficits grow, as that inflation zooms, as the ceiling on the national debt gets higher, as it is raised and raised again, the whole house of cards begins to tremble and even threatens to collapse. When and if that happens, guess who gets hit on the head. Guess who hurts! Guess who has to start all over again! It's not an abstraction called the government; it's you and me and it's our children and grandchildren. The government, no matter how unresponsive it may be, is ultimately us. That's why there is a fundamental fallacy in the way many of our irresponsible governors think about their jobs, and about their relationship to the American people. They seem to believe that they have a function unrelated to flesh and blood citizens and to the real world.

With all the talk about checks and balances, these irresponsible governors take actions in their public lives that they wouldn't dream of trying to pull off as private citizens.

There has been a widespread failure to respond to the fact that the actions of government have dramatic and lasting impact not only on society but on the individual lives of human beings who see their savings wiped away, their jobs going down the drain, and their futures shrivel before their eyes. The worst part of it is that the rhetoric of concern and compassion is used to justify acts without wisdom or care for the outcome of the Ponzi-like shenanigans that have passed as statesmanship until all too recently.

In the 1980's it will be impossible to combat any other social or economic problem until we wring out the inflation that threatens to drown our economy. The smugness of the fifties and sixties has been replaced in the White House and in Congress by panic and bewilderment. But if we had no reason to be smug then, we have no reason to panic now. We have the means to rid ourselves of inflation and to re-store stable growth to the economy. If we set realistic goals and take our medicine, we'll be on the road to economic health.

The medicine is the application of rational economic principles to a profound economic and social dislocation. Unfortunately, the patient (the American people) must also kick the habit of demanding instant gratification of all their social and political aspirations. Social Security is no security at all when the dollar is worth ten cents. Hospital care for the aged and needy is no care at all when the treasury is bare. Welfare payments and federal bailouts of great cities and giant companies will fail to staunch either human hurt or restore economic vitality if the dollars used are worthless in the marketplace. None of those things has come to pass yet. But the threat that any and all of them are possible has become dramatically obvious; and that offers us the oppor-tunity to do what must be done.

No one knows better than I that discussions of economic probity and calls for balanced budgets are the stuff of which snores are made. In politics some people call a long-winded speech a MEGO. That means "my eyes glaze over." But if I tell you that your bank is being held up, that your money is being stolen, that your house is being robbed, you'll wake up in a hurry. The fact is all of those things are in the process of happening, and the only burglar alarm that will do us any good is to put a rein on national appetites, to restore productivity to a level that will increase both jobs and goods during the next ten years, and to increase the savings and investment that will make all of this possible. None of these things can be done unless the others are done, too. If this political and social problem can be called a war (and that's what we seem to call most of the dilemmas that comprise the national agenda) then it's a three-front war. Many of the battles in those wars are fought in the trenches of the congressional committee system.

Public Works was my principal committee when I first came to the Senate. I chose that committee because it had jurisdiction over TVA, it had jurisdiction over the Army Corps of Engineers, which had control of the operation of the Cumberland River in Tennessee, and because it had primary jurisdiction over the newly emerging air- and water-pollution legislation. The committee system is the way that Congress acknowledges silently that it can't be expert in everything and creates specialists within its own ranks. We become specialists by force of exposure to expert testimony. If you prepare for those hearings with diligence it's a fairly prompt learning process.

I developed an early and favorable rapport with the Democrats and Republicans on the committee. Jennings Randolph of West Virginia has been there off and on since 1933. He was elected in 1932 and he's the only member remaining who went to the Congress the same day as my father-in-law, Senator Dirksen. Jennings is fond of reminding me of that from time to time. He still is chairman of the Public Works Committee and he does an extraordinarily effective job, although I think sometimes that the state of West Virginia is going to sink because of the weight of the federal projects that have gone there.

Ed Muskie is another committee member with extraordinary ability. His thoroughness and the careful approach he takes to air- and water-pollution control, a really new and complex subject, are great things to see.

Muskie is a scholarly type. He is forceful. He has a fiery, volcanic temper. He can rage at one moment and mediate the next, but he is always a loyal friend. He is a skillful senator, but more important than that, he's a sound and solid person. I've seen him withstand the most extraordinary type of pressure and abuse in public hearings, and in private, over the developing new air- and water-pollution legislation. It's important to bear in mind that the legislative battles over automobile emission-control systems were waged during the period in which we served on Public Works. Much of that time I was the senior member of the subcommittee. I can recall the acute harassment that came from the automobile industry about the necessity to do these things; and the arguments about whether smog was hurtful at all, and whether we ought to leave it up to the states or whether there should be a uniform system or whether we should have a special exemption for California or whether we should go with the catalytic converter.

Eddie Cole was president of GM at the time. Cole was a remarkable industrialist and a very insightful citizen. He came up with the idea of the catalytic converter and frankly he convinced Muskie and he convinced me that it was the way to go. Until this day that is a highly controversial issue. But I'm convinced that without the catalytic converter we never would approach the air-quality standards that we knew we needed then, and certainly know we need now. I think we have just about whipped automobile pollution. The remaining pollution, the haze you see in the atmosphere from 30,000 feet in an airliner, mostly comes now from the sulfur in the atmosphere generated by fossil-fueled electric generating plants. Like almost everything else in life, legislative problems involve conflicting objectives and trade-offs.

I've been in the Senate for twelve years now and more than once I've gone to committee meetings at which contradictory objectives were simultaneously and successfully pursued. The Tellico Dam Project is a perfect example of what I mean, and it's a good illustration of the kind of policy confusion that has come to plague us as government has grown bigger and more powerful.

Because I represent Tennessee in the Senate I am particularly interested in dams sponsored by the TVA. As a member of the Public Works Committee I also have a great interest in environmental issues. So this was a hard one for me to call. I've sponsored much of the legislation that's designed to protect natural resources, wildlife, and species that are threatened with extinction. One of those species is the snail darter. And one of the places where the snail darter lives just happened to be exactly where the Tellico Dam was being built. Thirteen years and $135 million had been spent on a project that was intended to provide industrial development in an economically depressed area, supply power sufficient for 20,000 homes, and serve as a recreational resource. Tennesseeans would have 7,000 jobs more when the Tellico Dam was completed, but, like everything else in life, the dam had its costs. In this case environmentalists contended that the snail darter would be wiped from the earth if the dam were completed. According to the dam's opponents there was no other place for the snail darter to go.

I don't know any human being living in Tennessee who has a single thing against the snail darter. They are very small, minnowlike creatures, and it's true that there are very few of them. That's why arrangements were made to lift them from their swimming hole near the dam site and put them into another area where the species could continue to flourish. But that wasn't nearly enough for the people who regard the environment as their special province. Legal action was instituted under the Endangered Species Act which resulted in a court decision that forbade the completion of the Tellico Dam. As a result, the economic climate in Tennessee (which really means the jobs and future well-being of my constituents) could have been hurt; the prospects for human growth would have been sacrificed in the name of an absolute principle that was not in fact being violated. The point is that a system built on compromise too frequently fails to make the trade-offs that are necessary to sustain itself. On the one hand, we're concerned with unemployment and productivity. But on the other hand, we are constrained by well-intentioned legislation and judicial fiat from common-sense decision-making. The Tellico Dam is one small symptom of government paralysis.

This particular story should have a happy ending. The snail darter now darts in a clear-water pool only three miles from its original home; the Tellico Dam is once again under construction, and the people who live in the area can look forward to the fulfillment of its economic promise. But it took the time and energies of the entire United States Senate, the House of Representatives, the TVA, the EPA, and at least six federal judges to resolve the issue.

We can't turn back the clock. Very few people living in this huge and complicated world of the eighties want to try to do so. But nostalgia is as old as the feeling Adam and Eve had after they were thrown out of the Garden of Eden. Even though we've never been in Eden, we're rightly convinced that our own past had qualities well worth preserving. We want to hold on to the values that have made us a free and a successful people at the same time we make those changes that are necessary to maintain and improve our condition. First we have to recognize that the government agency hasn't been invented that can pull a rabbit out of a hat. Too often we've convinced ourselves that government departments can and should do exactly that.

The Federal Reserve Board, called the central bank in

most other Western countries, is an important factor in determining how much money flows through the economy, where it goes, and where it doesn't go. It can make it possible for you to borrow, to spend, and to build an economic plant capable of reasserting American primacy as an industrial nation. It can bolster the dollar by its manipulations in the international exchange market; the Federal Reserve can also, as we have reason to know, take actions that tend to reduce the flow of money, raise its cost, contract our ability to buy a car or build a house, and reduce our ability to improve and expand our commercial plant. So the Federal Reserve chairman, whether he's a Republican or a Democrat, tends to make the headlines. Today it's Paul Volker. Yesterday it was Arthur Burns. Volker is an interesting figure. But for me Burns will always be the essence of the central banker. I have a high respect for him both as a person and as an economist. I think he was an extraordinarily good administrator of the Federal Reserve. He's an old-fashioned supply-and-demand free enterpriser.

He just believes in keeping an orderly bank, and he's a good banker. He is also a professor; he looks like a professor; he acts like a professor, and he used to treat me like a student! I encouraged that because I always profited from it. Occasionally, several times a year, Burns would call me or we'd see each other at a dinner party or a public function and he'd say, "It's time for us to have breakfast together. Why don't you come down next Tuesday at seven-thirty?" It was always stated with great exactitude, which is characteristic of the way he ran the Federal Reserve. After they built the new Federal Reserve Building I was intrigued with the fact that Arthur Burns stayed on in the old building. He felt the new one in some way an unseemly place for the chairman. The old one was richly paneled and done in supple leathers and old carpets. Usually there were only the two of us at breakfast, but occasionally Senator Henry Bellmon would join us. Arthur would push a little button that looked like a remote control on a television set and two waitresses would serve the same breakfast on every occasion. There was never an agenda, but Burns always had some particular subject on his mind.

He'd bite down on his pipe. His steel-rimmed glasses seemed to contract in size with the intensity of his gaze. He always looked straight ahead and almost never at me, except occasionally for punctuation. When Arthur started to lecture I had the overwhelming temptation to take notes. But I'd never taken notes very well in college so I resisted the impulse. Usually, as he went on, you'd find embedded in that lecture some particular point, sometimes involved with a particular piece of legislation that was or was about to be before the Congress, but more often than not some sort of observation on the way things were. He grew terribly impatient with Nixon early on. I recall seeing him a number of times at social functions during the Watergate period, and I could see the indignation seething. I was never sure that it was anger over a particular allegation or event as much as it was his feeling about the embarrassment to the institution and the disparagement of the process. He is a fiercely determined patriot. Arthur Burns is one of the few men I know who links economics to patriotism. He believes that free enterprise is so much an integral part of the American system that an assault on that or on the solidity of the dollar is in his view an unpatriotic act. His wife, Helen, has a strong personality. She is slight and demure, but she has a fiery intellect. When you're at a dinner party or some other social gathering where she's present, she's the only person there who can completely derail the rather ponderous logic that Burns occasionally spews in all directions. She can take that train right off the track.

But Helen Burns notwithstanding, the Federal Reserve Board in the person of its chairman has become, in the eyes of most of those who think about such matters, the arbiter of America's economic destiny.

I think that's plain wrong. It's wrong to think that way because by implication it means that we look to an unelected body to make our economic decisions for us. There's nothing democratic about that. You may have a friend at Chase Manhattan, as the TV commercials claim, but you shouldn't have a boss there.

The banking system, *Federal Reserve included,* is one of the principal factors in the way the economy works. It isn't, and it shouldn't be, the determining factor in what it does, or why and when it does it. And I'm sure Arthur Burns would agree with me.

What's true for the rest of the federal government is true for the Federal Reserve. It doesn't produce a thing. The only thing it manufactures is cheap or tight money. It is, in other words, one more unnatural barrier to free decisions in a free, productive marketplace. You and I, and the elected officials we send to Washington, and to state and city capitals all across the country, must make the hard decisions that determine our economic health.

Monetary policy as decided by the Federal Reserve Board is simply a reflection of the reality that we create when we pass spending bills, tax bills, and budgets. It's hard to believe, but for eleven years out of the last twelve, government has spent more than it has taken in. And in three out of the last four years that gap has steadily widened. There's no reason that the Federal Reserve's monetary policy must continue to reflect that kind of political reality. The time has come to take the future into our own hands. We have to force ourselves, that is we have to force our government, to do the painful budget cutting that will put your money back in your pockets, so that you can make your own decisions as to how and where to spend it.

We sometimes seem to be passengers in a leaky rowboat out in the middle of the lake. If we bail out in one spot, a hole springs up in another. That's why I believe the only way we're going to get a handle on our long-term spending spree is a constitutional amendment to limit federal government spending.

There are several ways in which this amendment can be written. But they all have one thing in common: *they all draw a constitutional line against excessive spending.* Let's face it. In one way it's a sad thing that we've reached a point where such an amendment is necessary. It's almost like saying we have to join Alcoholics Anonymous. But if that's what is necessary to break the habit, then that's what we have to do. How would it work?

4

Entitlements, Roller Coasters, and "the Baker Principle"

A constitutional amendment is no small matter. It is not to be undertaken lightly simply to facilitate what one group or another thinks is a desirable legislative objective. Actually, the first ten amendments were all passed in one fell swoop and in real terms have been part and parcel of the original document ever since the government began to function. When you look at it that way, the Constitution has been amended only sixteen times in two hundred years. The amending process went through all of the stages necessary for ratification only when fundamental issues that could be resolved in no other way appeared to threaten our political stability.

Just think about some of the great social questions that were ultimately settled by embodiment of new principles in the Constitution. The first ten amendments (or the Bill of Rights) were incorporated as a package by men who felt strongly that individual freedom must be protected against government itself. Freedom of assembly, the right to petition, freedom of religion, freedom of the press, the right to habeas corpus, and a number of other safeguards against the power of unbridled government were of the utmost concern to some of the very same men who drafted the original document.

Later amendments have usually reflected the changing needs and the changing mores of American society as it has grown from an infant republic to a continental giant. The Fourteenth Amendment extended the umbrella of due process of law to protect the individual citizen against the state as well as the federal government.

Members of the Senate were elected in the early days of the Republic by state legislatures. It wasn't until 1913 that the Constitution was amended to require direct election; and it was in the same year that it took a constitutional amendment to empower the government to levy an income tax. The men who passed the Sixteenth Amendment couldn't have known that they might be planting the seed for another amendment to alleviate the effects of the first one. But that has happened more than once. In 1919, after a wave of temperance reform, the American people applauded the passage of the Eighteenth Amendment prohibiting the use of alcoholic beverages. No one realized at the time that a well-intentioned attempt to change the personal habits of individual citizens would end up spinning the country through the Roaring Twenties. America took a bath in alcohol in the 1920's. It was against the law, and among many citizens Prohibition destroyed respect for the law. Fourteen years later Congress passed and the states ratified an amendment wiping out Prohibition. People literally danced in the streets. If anything in our history vividly demonstrates the importance of considering every aspect of the amending process, it is the almost farcical, and in many ways the tragic, results of the Eighteenth Amendment.

But there are other lessons to be learned, too. The passage of the Women's Suffrage Amendment, requiring for the first time that women be given the right to vote in federal and state elections, took place only after a long and bitter struggle. Ironically, it doubled the vote but did little to clean up politics in the way its proponents had expected. And, sixty years later, we are still in the midst of a struggle for fully equal rights for more than half of our population. The Equal Rights Amendment in 1980 is the center of the same kind of intense controversy that the right to vote stirred up in the early part of the century.

The amending process is a lightning rod for the social and political forces that have shaped society during every period of our history. Those amendments that actually make it through the long and bruising process established by the Constitution are usually the expression of such strong conviction that they become a kind of folk wisdom that provides the nation with its principal cultural safety valve. That valve should be turned only when countervailing forces are strong enough to block necessary social and political change through other means, and when unmanageable consequences are threatened if the environment isn't altered.

In the early 1980's runaway deficit spending has so disrupted America's economy and social life that a turn of the constitutional valve appears to be the only way to maintain political equilibrium. Deficit spending has become so ingrained as a national habit that it is almost impossible for a legislator to stand against the special-interest programs of his or her constituents. (And it's important to remember that every single human being has a special interest in something.)

There's an old saying in politics that in order to become a statesman, you have to be a politician first. There are very few issues on which a congressman or a senator feels completely free to separate himself from the interests of those who elect him. If a politician has to take too much heat, he'll melt away, only to be replaced by another politician who will read the lesson to mean that you shouldn't take any heat at all.

During my campaign for reelection in 1978 we were in

Lexington, Tennessee, and ended up with pickets on both sides of the ERA question. There was a group of women who were ferociously opposed to the ERA amendment, and another group in the same meeting who were just as strongly for it. That was not an infrequent thing. One time in Clarksville, Tennessee, we had a request to meet with an anti-ERA group. We set that up at the courthouse and when we got there we found an aggregation of pro-ERAers as well. We had a fiery question and answer session for a while, and I found myself sort of a referee because they ended up fussing at each other in the white heat of combat.

I believe that political theatrics can sometimes defeat the very ends you're trying to serve. Too many people don't want to recognize that fact of life. A lot of newspapermen and television commentators used to say during the Vietnamese War "Why doesn't so-and-so resign?" or "How can George Ball stay in the government?" There would be a chuckle and nudges and nods, implying that these men and women were selling out their principles because they stayed on despite serious differences with their superiors in government. But a politician, whether he is elected or appointed to high office, knows one thing very well: the day he puts on his hat and takes a walk he is permanently out to lunch. No one will look for him during that long lunch hour. He has lost all influence on events, and it is impossible to measure or to assess when that marginal influence might have played a significant role. That's why it is so difficult to resign on an issue of principle when just down the road there is always another principle to be defended.

Legislators, in particular, are caught on the horns of the dilemma. They usually reflect the overall views of the communities from which they've come, or else they wouldn't have arrived in the state capital or in Washington, D.C., in the first place. Like most of their constituents in the late seventies, they probably feel (in fact many of them campaigned on that feeling) that government is spending entirely too much money and that inflation has to stop. But few of them realize, until they get here, that it's easy to feel that way about the money being spent on somebody else. But it is tough, in fact in many cases it is impossible, to feel that way about the money spent on your friends and neighbors. The figures tell the story, and the figures are startling. In 1900 the federal government spent $141 million on programs designed to put money into individual pockets. Almost all of it was for veterans' benefits. Other programs were minuscule. In 1935 the figure was $374 million. Most of the money still went to the veterans. But in 1979 fully 57 percent of the federal budget of $547 billion was spent on entitlement programs. That means $315 billion were taken from the federal treasury and directly or indirectly placed in the pockets of over 100 million people. All of those people are voters or members of the families of voters. It is asking a good deal of a legislator to consistently vote against the large spending programs that appear to improve the lives of his constituents.

All spending programs make *someone* feel good. They have had a collective impact over the last century that goes far beyond the individual effects of the particular appropriation and its expenditure. The most cursory kind of rundown of "special spending" by the federal government includes the entire range of America's social, corporate, and labor interests. Just over the last five or six years we have enacted in Washington a food-stamp program that began by spending $2.2 billion to assist poor people who could not otherwise afford a decent diet and that expanded to include citizens with incomes of $11,000 per year. The annual cost today is just under $7 billion and rising. A good many of these people we expected in times past to supply their own wants. In 1975, and again in 1979, we enacted legislation to put federal funds at the disposal of New York City. These funds were needed because of economic decisions taken in New York City by elected officials that simply could not be sustained by New York's economic base. In 1972 the federal government bailed out Lockheed Aircraft, one of the great examples of the private enterprise system. Almost simultaneously, we gave the largest handout in history to the Penn Central Railroad, and we have expanded our Social Security system to embrace 35 million recipients. In 1979 we saw the spectacle of Chrysler Motors, the third largest automobile manufacturer in the world, asking for federal loan guarantees well in excess of $1.5 billion. In each and every one of the above instances there was good and sufficient reason for the United States government to be deeply concerned about the needs of those to whom we gave the money. There is more than one kind of welfare in this country, and we have built a structure in which government has come to be deeply involved in distributing the funds for that welfare.

Since World War II we have developed an "entitlement" psychology. That's something like having a "proprietary interest" in your job (a concept that has actually been validated by legal decision in the federal courts). But such entitlements and proprietary interests can become inordinately expensive when the books never balance.

A good example is the situation in which New York City landlords have abandoned buildings by the thousands because they were no longer economically viable. When these landlords walk away from their own property the social costs are staggering to the people who live in the South Bronx, for instance, and they're economically devastating to a city that depends on property tax for much of its revenue. Such results are inevitable when resources are stretched beyond their capacity.

Why is it so difficult to put a rein on expenditures that we obviously can't afford? Believe it or not, the fact that politicians like to be reelected to office is only one of the many factors that has brought us to a point where we have to consider seriously a constitutional limit on federal spending. But it is something to remember.

Joe Evins was a congressman from Tennessee, a Democrat, and he and my father had served together. After I arrived in the Senate, Joe became the dean of the Tennessee delegation. He was subcommittee chairman of the Public Works Appropriations Subcommittee. That meant that he had a good deal to say about where and when public buildings would be put up.

The Tennessee legislature, in its infinite wisdom, had transferred my county and the adjoining county into Joe Evins' Democratic district. Those two counties were heavily Republican and it terrified Joe Evins, who'd been there forever and saw the first glimmer of trouble to his political career and his political security. So he made whirlwind tours through those counties. He hatched post offices everywhere he went. He ordered post offices for Morgan County, Scott County, and Fentress County. One day he called me and said, "Howard, I want to see that you have a new federal building in your hometown of Huntsville." You have to keep in mind Huntsville had a population of 374 people at the last census, my first year in the Senate. I said, "Joe, I really don't want a new post office in Huntsville. I don't think we need one. I appreciate it but we don't need one." About a week later I got a phone call from the administrator of the General Services Administration. He said, "Do you want that post office to be in brick or stone?" And I said I had told Congressman Evins that we don't really need a post office. He said, "That's not what I asked. You're gonna get the damn post office. Now, do you want brick or stone?"

The political process itself is responsible for much of the difficulty. When a program is proposed in Congress with any significant support there, it is the crystallization of a good deal of support back home; and "back home" means back home in all or most parts of the country. When that program is discussed in committee and debated on the floor, its virtues are emphasized. The positive aspects of its passage are underlined. The opposition, by the very necessity of opposing, appears negative. There is a quality of rearguard action to the maneuvers of those who say "no." To put it simply, no one likes to spoil a party.

When the measure is passed, it becomes part of the law of the land. Its very passage creates a brand-new series of constituencies. First, of course, the recipients of the program's benefits become deeply committed to its survival. The administrators of the program must be its advocates if they are to be effective. They in turn build organizations to develop the program, and to fulfill all of its needs. The suppliers of material, contractors, and consultants all become part of a new entity that depends for its life on money from the federal exchequer.

Every new program is the foundation for institution building, and institutions are notoriously reluctant to end their own lives. There is always a reason to continue a program, even when a good case can be made that its objective has been served, or that it no longer fulfills a useful social function. Individual lives become at least partially rooted in all of these programs, and the people affected will fight with more passion to sustain them than their opponents can usually marshal in opposition. We have reached a point where it is necessary to ask ourselves how we can bring this most severe problem in our domestic lives under control.

The real question is one of cost and structure. That's not necessarily the same as "cost effectiveness" or "cost-benefit ratio"; it does mean that we must find a way to accomplish a great many socially desirable ends without the investment of full-scale social-political-financial commitment by the national government. We may have reached the point where taxation for entitlement means the reduced economic growth that carries with it the probability of individual pain and social instability. But I believe that there is no way we can be exact about when that point is reached. I have, however, evolved the "Baker Principle." It says, "When you ride a roller coaster that's out of control, you want to get off."

I believe we're riding that roller coaster now. I believe that's why we must put on the brakes in the form of a constitutional amendment. It's time for the process to correct itself.

In the political landscape of 1979 it was necessary to take a dramatic first step on the road to reforming the federal spending machine. That's why I co-sponsored, with Senator Richard Lugar, a constitutional amendment that would prevent Congress from appropriating more funds in any given year than actually came into the federal treasury during the same period. Only a two-thirds vote by both Houses of Congress could eliminate that requirement. The Lugar Amendment is a realistic device that raises the action of deficit spending to a deliberate act rather than an accident. A two-thirds majority decision to do so would have the same constitutional impact as overriding a presidential veto. This amendment, while it retains the flexibility to meet economic reality, imposes a constitutional discipline on spending that has been lacking for much too long a time. It would take a whale of a national emergency to get two-thirds of Congress to agree on anything. But our spending habits had become so threatening to the economy that it was necessary to "get their attention."

In a national emergency the constitutional prohibition would be lifted. But we would no longer be passengers on that runaway roller coaster.

5

That "Fed-up Feeling" and Political Shell Games

It's hardly a secret that the tax burden most Americans bear has increased steadily in the last fifteen years. The proposal to limit spending by constitutional fiat in part reflects the growing unease of Americans with the staggering tax burdens they have come to expect, if not accept.

Today, the average American family of four, earning about $18,000 a year, pays nearly $4,000 in federal taxes. If that family lives in a high-tax state or city, it may pay as much as 15 percent of its gross income. When it's all put together, that's a terrific drag on the U.S. economy. Money that would otherwise be spent on consumer goods or saved and invested for the future is sucked into the vacuum cleaner of the federal treasury.

If we're not careful we may explode our favorite myths about the American character. We say we believe in the work ethic, and that a penny saved is a penny earned. Unfortunately, the habits of modern life have worn away the basis for that belief. Today, almost unbelievably, the American people save less than the citizens of any other country in the West. Only 1 percent of the gross national product in 1979 went to savings. That's the price we pay for inflation. But it's also the price we pay for fear. The impulse to buy now and save later is rooted in the feeling that we can't count on tomorrow. It's as though a future-oriented people have suddenly decided that there's going to be no future at all. A conflict between belief and action, and between the habits of the past and the way we behave today, is simply an expression of creeping and increasingly pervasive uncertainty.

The antitax movement that hit California with the passage of Proposition 13 and the surge of similar proposals in other places is an expression of that feeling of unease. It's what I call the "fed-up feeling." And taking an aspirin won't make it go away. As a matter of fact, the fed-up feeling, as expressed in these tax-limiting movements, is probably the best medicine Americans can administer to this society. The results of Proposition 13 offer a perfect example of the difference between what politicians said would happen and what the majority of the people believed would happen. As is often the case, and as politicians too frequently forget, the people were right. The threatened cutbacks in service failed to materialize. The gloomily forecast economic slowdown turned into a surge of growth, and the unemployment predicted by politicians with a vested interest in big government never occurred. Proposition 13 was a test-tube case in which people insisted on translating the abstract principle of self-government into its flesh and blood reality.

The referendum is a sharp tool and, in this case, it should have served as a warning to other cities, states, and to the United States government itself. But it's really unimportant whether or not an individual politician or group of politicians was embarrassed because the voters overruled them on an important judgment. What's important is the fact that so many people in the business of government were in error about the fundamental principles on which a private enterprise economy is based. When it became apparent that the voters were intent on forcing their will, too many public officials shouted, "The sky is falling, the sky is falling!" And too few recognized that there's more than one way to govern a state.

The sky didn't fall as a result of Proposition 13; if anything, it cleared some of the smog of self-deception from the horizon. Business improved in California; people who left public employment moved into productive jobs; the tax base broadened and essential services were maintained, and in some cases improved.

Even in 1979 when the doom and gloom prophets among the economists forecast "mild recession" . . . "moderate recession" . . . "severe recession" . . . "worldwide depression" . . . the gross national product continued to grow. Finally, when the disease of confusion spread and the recession actually occurred, it was a result of the tight money policies forced on the Federal Reserve System by a government that competed in the money markets with its own citizens in order to pay the bills that came due in the wake of a $30 billion deficit.

The money markets are a mystery to most Americans. But they operate on the same principle as other economic forces. The high bidder gets the goods and no one can outbid the United States government when the government bids high enough. The cost of money forces business to delay the purchases it must make for new plant inventory, new supplies, and to employ those who need jobs. That's one of the most important reasons for restraint in government spending. The cost of money, or interest rates, climbs out of sight when the government soaks up the supply and then prints more money and then soaks that up, too. The dollar weakens in value at the very same time it increases in price.

We are getting a fast shuffle from a deck of cards dealt by government agents who have lost control of federal programs and the bureaucracy that administers them.

The most shocking evidence for a view that many of us have held for years was recently offered by a study sponsored by the federal government itself. This commission was created by Congress to study the relationship among federal, state, and local governments. In the fall of 1979 this is what its senior analyst, David R. Beam, had to say: "In numerous instances, program costs have soared beyond the expectations of the public officials who voted for them. For this reason, the construction of the contemporary leviathan state must be judged in part to be simply a mistake."

Some mistake!

"As government grows," Mr. Beam wrote, "this process of misjudgments is compounded by a kind of 'feedback mechanism.' The opportunity for further error becomes more numerous, more serious, and more costly."

Beam gave some graphic examples of his findings to *The New York Times*.

Item: In 1977 an apparently minor amendment was voted by Congress into the Small Business Administration's Disaster Loan Program, making farmers as well as businessmen eligible for benefits. The program was budgeted at $20 million, but within several months applications from farmers came to $1.4 billion.

Item: When Congress enacted disability insurance in 1956, sponsors estimated that costs by 1980 would be $860 million for one million workers. But the costs surpassed that figure *in the 1960's*. From 1970 to 1978 costs quadrupled to about $13 billion and for 1980 there are expected to be 5.4 million beneficiaries on the rolls, more than five times the original estimate.

Such examples of cost overruns and of overgovernment and overregulation can be cited ad nauseum. It's time to do something about it; and it's time to recognize that because the dollars you earn are needed to pay the government's bills, there is a deep-seated reluctance to cut taxes, even by policy-makers who are fully aware that a reduced tax burden is the most effective way to restore economic vitality.

In 1962, John F. Kennedy proposed and Congress accepted the kind of tax cut that we need even more in 1980.

In the early sixties that tax reduction resulted in an almost immediate rise in business investment to well over 10 percent of the annual gross national product. At the same time, that tax reduction enriched the American people to such an extent that the tax revenues themselves increased by over 50 percent within five years. And the value of the dollar inflated by slightly more than *one half of 1 percent*. But the years that followed were a very different story. The attempt to wage war in Vietnam and to expand government spending at home, at one and the same time, pushed us toward chronic stagflation. Whatever the differences among us about the Vietnamese War, there was no excuse to try and hide its cost. It was even worse to use the psychology of "guns *and* butter" on people who would eventually understand that they were unwitting victims of a political shell game.

6

What Must Be Done

Lincoln was right when he said you can't fool all of the people all of the time. But he didn't reckon with another less pleasant aspect of human behavior. The emperor usually believes he's fully dressed, and when he's told he has no clothes on he takes it personally. Too many of the "spend now, pay maybe" lawmakers truly believe that the financial reckoning can be indefinitely postponed. It's something like Judgment Day. It could happen. Who knows?

Scarlett O'Hara summed it up nicely: "I'll think about that tomorrow."

In 1980 the bill has been presented; and we have to begin to pay it *on the installment plan.* It would be irresponsible in the extreme to contend that any administration can or should indiscriminately eliminate the consequences of thirty years of incredible growth in government expenditure. Some of those consequences have been positive, and have become so embedded in our way of life that it would be impossible to erase them in any acceptable way.

Those of us who are committed to fiscal responsibility and careful assessment of government involvement in the everyday life of the citizenry must see to it that the mandate of the American people is honored and that the obligations of the federal government are met in a rational way. What is useful must be retained; what is wasteful must be pruned. Our political leaders must respond to the message from every part of the country that there are new and specific expectations about the way Washington should work. The people who pay the bills are demanding efficient and effective administration of programs to aid the needy, cushion the frightening effects of unemployment, to provide access to the most advanced health care in the world, and to assist in the improvement of our educational system.

Every one of these objectives can be achieved if we bite the bullet of accountability. Program dollars must be clearly related to tax dollars actually in the treasury, or on the way. That's the best and, really, the only reason for that constitutional amendment to restrain spending.

Program services must be regularly evaluated to see whether or not it's time for a "mission accomplished" and a shutdown, or whether it is necessary to continue the program in the same way. Judgments must be made on whether the program's objectives should be altered or whether the mission was badly conceived in the first place. When programs no longer can be justified let's put them into the history books!

One way to achieve these objectives is the "sunset law." Another is called "zero-based budgeting." When President Carter was elected in 1976, he proposed to put both of these concepts to work. Under the sunset law a program would automatically go out of existence in two, three, or five years unless Congress could be convinced that it was still necessary to accomplish an important end. Zero-based budgeting is a method whereby a government agency must establish in numerical order what it regards as its most important priorities. Every dollar it spends must be justified each year. In other words, every program must start from scratch at the beginning of every fiscal year. To my knowledge, the sun has yet to set on a single federal program. Zero-based budgeting may have turned the hair gray on many a bureaucratic head, but the costs of federal programs certainly have been totally unaffected.

It's only fair to say that Congress has been reluctant to apply sunset laws because experience teaches that the bureaucracy will spend most of its time preparing to justify its existence rather than in implementing the programs for which it's responsible. There's enough pretense and shadow-boxing in the cubbyholes of official Washington without adding to the gamesmanship. That does not mean that the problem is insoluble. In a representative democracy, the men and women elected to make the laws are best suited to see to it that they are faithfully executed. That's why the concept of congressional oversight should be expanded during these next years. Under such conditions zero-based budgeting can become more than bureaucratic gamesmanship.

When I used the phrase "the irresponsible governors" I had in mind the high-ranking civil servants who administer the laws passed by Congress. It is up to these people and their subordinates, who have chosen government as their profession, to interpret the law and to write the rules (in government jargon they're called "the regs") that appear in the *Federal Register.*

These men and women have wide latitude in deciding what Congress means them to do. They spread across the land and investigate whether you and I (or whoever is affected by a particular regulation) are obeying the rules. Those who stay in Washington, or in any one of the dozen federal buildings throughout the country while others are "in the field," decide who is eligible to receive federal funds appropriated by Congress in connection with laws affecting farmers, businessmen, school systems, local and state governments, and hundreds of other private and public interests. All too frequently the decisions are made on arbitrary or arcane or outrageous grounds. The bureaucrats have more than once successfully invoked the aid of the federal courts in the ongoing attempt to expand their power. Their compulsive intrusiveness seeps into every corner of the political system.

When Nelson Rockefeller was governor of New York he imposed a rule that required welfare recipients to appear personally in order to receive their benefit checks. The idea was to assist recipients in finding work, and to cut down on the state's zooming welfare expenditures. The Department of Health, Education, and Welfare intervened and went to federal district court to insist that the welfare clients had a right to receive their funds by mail. HEW lawyers cited its own rules (those little *Federal Register* numbers) as proof that when Congress passed welfare legislation it intended to prevent the states from imposing the kind of rules that New York had just invoked.

Governor Rockefeller got on the telephone with Wilbur Mills and Russell Long, the chairmen of the committees that had jurisdiction, and asked them if the HEW boys had it right. The fact was that HEW had completely misconstrued congressional intent. Congress had meant to make it possible for the states to pass just such belt-tightening legislation! HEW had written regulations contravening the intent of Congress and then pointed to them as evidence of a fictional legislative history.

This was one of those rare occasions when the bureaucrats were caught out. A colloquy between Senator Long and Senator Buckley on the floor of Congress made it very clear as to what Congress had in mind and the HEW case was thrown out on appeal. This rule of the mandarins was the ruin of ancient China. And it is one of the most pernicious effects of the big government of our own day.

But we have a built-in antidote if we choose to use it. The President and Congress can cooperate to reduce the bureaucratic role in rulemaking and evolve a process in which congressional intent is judged and effected by Congress itself.

Much of today's congressional oversight consists of "show and tell," in which cabinet officers and agency heads justify their activities in connection with a hearing on appropriations. When Congress is dealing with whether and how much money to appropriate, it commands its most respectful attention from the executive branch.

But the Constitution intends much more than that for Congress. And it anticipated no policy-making role at all for a bureaucracy that has developed into the fourth branch of government.

If the twentieth century has brought us new problems it offers new solutions as well. When my father went off to serve his first term in Congress back in 1950, he spent less than six months a year in Washington. Congress would go into session in December, pass whatever laws were necessary, and go home in May. (It may have had something to do with the lack of air conditioning, but going home for six months or more had much to be said for it.)

I think my father wanted all of his life to serve in the House of Representatives. I remember that when I was a young man he had an almost idolatrous attitude toward J. Will Taylor, who was a great congressman from the Second District. Will served for many years. He drove a long, gray Studebaker automobile. One time he was driving through Huntsville and somebody rear-ended the congressman. The fellow fairly flew out of the car shouting, "Why didn't you signal that turn?" Will Taylor looked him up and down, and if there's such a thing as hearing icicles drip from a man's voice, that's when I heard them drip. "You damn fool, if you can't see anything as big as this car, how are you going to see anything as small as my hand?"

J. Will Taylor was quite an act to follow. But my father was more than adequate to the job. He paid close attention to his constituents and he regarded his service in Congress as the capstone of his career.

I was eight years old when my mother died. My father's remarriage brought into my life another parent dedicated to the public service. In my family we had Congresspersons of both sexes. After my father's death, she succeeded to his seat. They were both genuinely *citizen legislators*. They and their colleagues had roots in their home communities that were strengthened by close and constantly renewed ties. They went home and lawyered or doctored or managed a business, or just talked to their neighbors for half of every year.

Because Congress is now tied to Washington for almost all of every year we have become elected bureaucrats, further and further removed from the places and the people who sent us to Washington. That's an occupational hazard that I refuse to accept. I return to my home in Huntsville, Tennessee, almost every week I can. But many simply can't make that kind of regular journey. It's a problem that can and must be remedied; and the problem of the irresponsible governors can be solved at the same time.

Congress must change the emphasis on what and how it does its job. Instead of making so many new laws, the legislative branch should concentrate on those laws that are already on the books. In the 1980's an American President who wants to get the job done will ask Congress to send its representatives as observers of the agency rulemaking process. That's the kind of open government that will enable the legislative branch to have the facts on which an agency has made a decision based on law.

If the American people are to maintain their confidence that this government is responsive to their will, their elected representatives must begin to play a more active role in those government activities that have direct effects on the lives of individual citizens.

Congress must go to the country.

I propose a break with the procedures of the past that have become so encrusted with age that they no longer assist in getting the job done. In the 1980's the Congress of the United States should split the legislative year into two parts. Members would arrive in Washington in January, stay for four months, and consider the substance of whatever new laws they think are in the public interest. At that point the members would go back home, just like in the old days, to listen to their constituents, to oversee the work related to their committee responsibilities, and to listen to new ideas.

Then, in the fall of the year, there would be another session held in Washington to be devoted only to the appropriation of funds for carrying on the government's work.

This is a simple and effective device to prevent the legislative logjams that so often gum up the works under the present cumbersome system. The appropriations process could no longer be used to get a particular pet project passed or to prevent funds from being appropriated as a way to block the will of the majority. Money bills would be considered on their merits alone; and new laws would be passed when members of Congress were fresh from close contact with the people the laws affect. Legislators would again be *citizen* legislators, and a sense of immediacy and responsiveness would be restored to the process.

Rather than spend all of its time in the Capitol, Congress must recognize that there is enormously useful work to be done in supervising the interpretation and implementation of laws that it makes. I believe the congressional oversight hearings must be sharpened as a tool of government. If the Federal Trade Commission imposes regulations under the umbrella of congressional legislation, then the congressional committees that have shaped that legislation should see at firsthand its effect on the American people. If, under the cover of law, regulations are established that affect how wheat is harvested, or how drugs are sold over the counter, or what labels are required for food stuffs, or the distance between machines in an industrial plant, then the members of Congress who have made it all possible should get out there and see how well these regulations work. The only reliable way to establish the efficacy of what we do in Washington is to see what the people think of the nitty-gritty we have put into their lives.

A combination of this kind of intensive legislative oversight, taking up much of the congressional work year, when linked to a congressional presence at agency headquarters, will make for a much more responsive bureaucracy and, just as important, a much more responsive legislature. I have a hunch that once the isolation of the Senate and House chambers is penetrated by the day-to-day reality of contact with the people we represent, we will exercise much greater care about the nature and number of the laws we make. The American people will come to have a great deal more confidence in representatives who are obviously alert to their interests and concerns. Interaction between government and people is the essence of a successful democratic society.

But, no matter what Congress alone does, the incontrovertible fact is that millions of people simply don't know how to respond to the massive government involvement that impacts on their lives in such pervasive ways. There is too frequently a sense of loss of control that eventually results in resentful passivity. I wrote earlier of the indifference that expresses itself in "staying home from politics." One of the most effective ways to combat that attitude is to remove the sense of distance between government and people. That's a job the President of the United States must begin immediately. He should take measures to bring the enormous and faceless bureaucracy in charge of government's day-to-day actions closer to the realities of the community it serves. These "irresponsible governors" are irresponsible only because they are unaccountable. There is no counterbalance to the anonymity of the bureaucratic power structure.

I'm fairly certain that the resentment people feel toward big government is not so much that government does too much (although it *does* do too much) but rather that most of the things that government does are done through the work of an anonymous bureaucracy. The American colonists used to rail against taxation without representation; but I would suspect that what really annoyed them was not the tariff on tea. It was, rather, the simple fact that they couldn't see and they didn't know the people who imposed the burden of taxation. They couldn't locate them. They couldn't vote for them or against them; and they wouldn't know them if they passed them on the street. The American colonies were a possession. The British Parliament was anonymous. And that description applies remarkably well to the structure of much of our own government in the late twentieth century.

Too many of the decisions that affect your life in a very real way are made by strangers. Whether it's the size of your paycheck and the number of groceries you can buy, whether you can remain independent in your later years are questions determined by people you never heard of. You haven't the foggiest notion where they are located. Like those colonists who threw the tea overboard in Boston Harbor, you can't vote for them and you can't vote against them. The frustration quotient is extraordinary.

To remove the quality of anonymity, to open up the system of government is a major challenge. If we shed our preconceptions the problem can be solved.

In 1981 the next President should propose and Congress should institute a federal magistrate system to represent individual citizens in their contacts with the executive branch. Such magistrates would be chosen to interface with agencies ranging from the Social Security Administration to the Veterans Administration, to the Department of Education, or to the Department of Health, Education, and Welfare. Any ordinary citizen living in Ames, Iowa, who has a problem that should be addressed by one of the federal departments would no longer be confronted with the feeling that in order to get anything done a person must wander through the labyrinth of Kafka's *Castle*. We forget too often that federal instructions are written in jargon unintelligible to ordinary human beings. Federalese has replaced the English language in government usage, and most Americans are unacquainted with that usage.

The technicalities of whom to deal with and what to ask for to solve a personal problem are often staggering to people unacquainted with government's procedures. In the old days (that is before we reformed the party system right out of the business of helping people), an old person, a sick person, or someone short of money could turn to the political machine for assistance in cutting through the inevitable red tape. That, unfortunately, is no longer the case in most places in this country. When we removed the machinery of politics from its direct relation to government, we removed a comforting and useful cushion effect on which millions of people had come to rely.

Reform has its costs. The bureaucrats who are necessary to run the system simply don't have the same feeling about the citizenry they serve as did the oldstyle politicians. In fact, I sometimes get the feeling that some members of the briefcase brigade truly believe that they are responsible only to themselves. They think that Congress is an obstacle to be bypassed or torpedoed when it occasionally puts in its oar on behalf of its constituents. I recently had an experience that almost made the smoke come through my ears. It illustrates the failure of the bureaucracy to understand that Congress represents the people and that one of the bureaucracy's most important functions is to assist Congress in that function.

Freed Hardeman is a little college in Henderson, Tennessee, and it's my job to assist institutions like it to receive the federal funds they deserve. I hope and expect every one of you has a congressman or senator who does that job for the schools in your district. When I was asked by the president of this little college to help put a grant through the monstrous labyrinth at HEW, I instructed my staff to get on the job. They shepherded the dean, David Thomas, through the maze and the school came out with a grant of something over $250,000. I should say here that Senator Jim Sasser, a Democrat and my Tennessee colleague, also put in a senatorial oar. In the House of Representatives that little school had friends like Robin Beard and Carl Perkins, members of different parties but each interested in that district and in getting its problems solved. But we had done our jobs as the people's surrogates a little too effectively to suit the anonymous bureaucrats. A flurry of leaked documents (that implied all sorts of skullduggery had been committed on behalf of little Freed Hardeman) hit the front pages of one of the Washington newspapers. The man who processes grants at HEW didn't like the order he had received from his superior to give the money to this little southern college; he screamed "foul" and strongly suggested that something illegal had been done. What had been done was to suggest that the senators from Tennessee and the congressmen from that school's district wanted adequate federal assistance for that little school. When the aid was granted, this particular irresponsible governor took it into his head that such interest by the congressional representatives of the people in that school constituted improper pressure. It never entered that bureaucrat's mind that Americans send representatives to Congress to represent their interests. In his heart of hearts that fellow knew that it was his job to obstruct those efforts. If a roadblock can prevent the people getting back some of their own money, why, let's pull it across the road!

Fortunately, Freed Hardeman got its funding on the merits; the students at that school were lucky that there were congressional staffers who cared enough to see it through.

For every incident like that one there are hundreds in which American citizens are blocked from meaningful access to responsible government officials by rules that come out of a sausage-making machine. In the 1980's, Congress needs help to help the people. The *bureaucracy is its own constituency,* and we need new institutions to replace those that have been destroyed by progress. The federal magistrate system offers just such an opportunity. Instead of the need to inquire in a dozen different places about what to do and how to do it, an ordinary American would simply discuss the problem with a man or woman whom he knows as a neighbor. For the magistrates would be selected on the basis of, among other things, their personal relationship to the communities in which they live. Their principal responsibility would be to facilitate the business of their neighbors with government. I don't want to imply that an adversary relationship should or would exist between these magistrates and the federal bureaucracy. On the contrary, the magistrate would serve both parties by bridging the gap between citizen and administrator.

He would be a problem solver and, at the same time, when and if the circumstances were appropriate, he would be an advocate of the interests of the citizen doing business with his government. The irresponsible governors would no longer be irresponsible, because in the nature of things they would recognize an accountability to the magistrate. Their actions, their identities, and the rationale for their decisions would all be a part of the record which the magistrate had assisted in making.

These magistrates would not be judges in robes sitting in impressive courtrooms. They would be more like rural mail carriers: people who are visible and known as the government's emissary to *you,* on your block, in your neighborhood. The magistrate would know how to work inside the system, and the people in that neighborhood would know where to find him. Perhaps they would have some limited power to stay a regulation's effect for a short time. But the principal job would be to remove the cloak of anonymity from the bureaucracy. This kind of human connection be-tween ordinary people and the too frequently forbidding institutions of government can make a substantial and pos-itive difference in the way we conduct our affairs. But it is only a single step in that process.

Washington, a city located on the eastern seaboard of a republic that spans three thousand miles of continent, is hardly the geographic or cultural center of the nation. Yet in two hundred years of history it has become richly en-dowed as the fullest expression of our political institutions. Millions of people from all parts of North America pour through the capital every year. To them it's what this coun-try is all about. And so it should remain. However, just as we can take government to the people, we can take parts of its symbolic expression as the capital to other parts of the country.

America's diversity is staggering. Departments of govern-ment located in Washington, D.C., often have principal functions that are tied directly to geographic areas far re-moved from the capital. I believe that we should begin to decentralize some of those functions that are now located in the District of Columbia and take them to where they belong.

The nation's heartland in the Midwest is also the center for much of its agricultural wealth. Newspaper readers, listeners to the radio, and television viewers in Iowa or Kan-sas or Nebraska see and hear much that has to do with farm-ing, its problems, its opportunities, and the style of life that agriculture generates. It is only appropriate, then, to send part of the Department of Agriculture (its assistant secre-taries, its commissioners, and its high administrators) to the American heartland. It is there that the real work is done. Let's put some of our offices where the farms and factories are.

Such arrangements could be made in many or most of the

departments of government. As an example, the Department of the Interior deals principally with public lands. Two thirds of the lands owned by the United States government are in the western and the southwestern parts of this country. Much of the apparatus of the Department of the Interior should be located in the same places. The Department of Commerce deals, among other things, with commodity markets, import and export licensing regulations, and a range of similar activities. Let's take those functions of government and put them in the places in which they naturally belong. There's room in Chicago, Illinois, for several more federal buildings and bureaucrats. If their jobs deal with the business of the people of Chicago they'll be welcome. Furthermore, I believe that they will do that job more effectively.

The departments of government are designed in significant part to represent constituencies. There is no reason for them to be separated from these constituencies by thousands of miles. That separation is far too often more significant than distance imposed by geography. There is a cultural divide between those who live in the isolation of the splendid capital and those who are governed by its regulations. That isolation must be breached for the good health of the Republic.

Proposals such as these are as significant as reminders of the problems that produce them as they are in and of themselves. The necessity for closer ties between the governors and the governed is expressive of a widening gulf between the viewpoints of the Washington elites and the people who sent them to Washington in the first instance. But violent cultural change in response to what we perceive as growing alienation may itself produce unforeseeable consequences that we would find even more unacceptable than things as they are.

The Capitol of the United States is in Washington, D.C., and its principal officers in the executive branch must remain here. For they are responsible to the President and they are accountable to Congress, and in that sense Washington is where it's at!

Still, we live in a period in which technology makes possible the effective linkage between the seat of government in Washington and its high representatives across the country. Telecommunications have reached a point of such sophistication and efficiency that continuous and instantaneous interplay between an assistant secretary in Des Moines and an undersecretary in Washington is as simple as the flick of the proverbial switch.

Recommendations such as these will seem to some people to smack of gimickry. I think that is because the use of technology as a means to achieve desirable social and political ends is still culturally alien to us, even as we approach the end of the twentieth century. Our knowledge of what is possible is very distant from the emotional and intellectual heritage that has shaped our character. The culture gap between what is and what could easily be is not readily bridged. It is difficult to absorb the reality that this is the generation that sent men to the moon. Some of them even came back to the Senate.

It's almost unbelievable, but it's true that astronauts as a class are the most overrepresented group in the country. They have 2 percent of the Senate. And they are extraordinary. The rest of us stand in awe and I think they know that. It's probably even more the case with Jack Schmitt than John Glenn because Schmitt not only was an astronaut; he bamboozled his way into the program. He had to learn how to fly after he got there. Schmitt had a Ph.D. in geology from Harvard and was already a distinguished geologist before he went into the program. He drives a pickup truck with a camper on the back. As far as I can see, the Senate has had zero impact on Schmitt. He is still a New Mexico geologist with a Harvard degree who's been to the moon and drives a pickup. That's 90 percent of Jack Schmitt.

Ten percent is senator. I believe that's predective of the future.

I think you're going to see fewer and fewer Senator Stennis types or Jennings Randolph types, and that isn't meant to diminish either one of them. It's to say that they're of an earlier time when the demands were not easier, but different. You're going to see more John Glenns and Jack Schmitts, whether they're industrialists, as with Chuck Percy, or merchants, as with Rudy Boschwitz. Rudy made a fortune before he came to the Senate, as a merchant who had an intuitive understanding of how to use intensive TV promotion to sell his product. Rudy himself is a product of his age. Using its tools comes naturally to him. I think you're going to see more self-made men, more pickup trucks with campers on them, and fewer limousines, and I think that's good. It's going to go a long way toward redemocratizing the Congress. It's one of the many ways that government has to reflect the changing nature of the people it represents.

A government that plays such a large role in the lives of the people should be among the people. Cooperation among all elements of the American system is more important today than it has ever been before. Government must break the habits of attitude that have dominated it for too long if it is to retain the allegiance of a people committed at one and the same time to efficiency and to self-rule.

Part II
What This Country Needs...

7

Old Band-Aids and the "New Economics"

At the beginning of the eighties most Americans are uncertain about the way to conduct their lives. Countless millions of decisions about what to buy, how much to save, where to invest, whether and how to plan for the long-range career goals and social aspirations are all related to the economic health of this society. There is an almost schizophrenic quality to the way we perceive our relationships to the economy. During the last fifty years fundamental changes in the way the citizen relates to economic institutions and in the way government relates to the citizen and to the economy have come to determine much about the quality of our lives.

The deep-seated commitment to free and private enterprise which we profess as a basic social value is today only a partial expression of the American reality. Whether or not we like it, government has come to play a dominant role in the way economic decisions are made. The free market is no longer as free as it once was. Federal and state regulation of industry and commerce has added significantly to the economic costs of doing business. The question of a particular regulation's value is only a single aspect of a situation in which the added costs imposed by federal domination of the process have distorted the natural interplay of economic forces.

It was during the seizure of the Great Depression of the 1930's that the so-called New Economics became a powerful governing force. World War II was the vehicle for its surge into a position of dominant influence on the economic process, and a generation of Americans grew up in a world in which new expectations of government were built into their perceptions of a free society. Those expectations are considerably different from the demands placed on government in earlier times. There is no good reason to believe that the situation has changed as a result of the great inflation that now threatens social stability. We must begin to absorb and understand the effect that this new economics has had on that stability and to make choices based on that understanding.

First, how and why did depression and war bring about such a fundamental change in the political and economic structure? It's important to raise this question if only because right now we are confronting a situation of equivalent threat. Our earlier experience may illustrate what we can expect if the economy unlooses forces that are harmful to many millions of people. How to apply the lessons of the past may illuminate the future.

For most of our history, government intervened little in the economy. Only when great social forces had to be tapped in the name of progress was government involvement required; and then simply to clear the way. I'm thinking in particular of the giant railroad systems that threw a great steel grid across America. Government cleared the way by exercising its right of eminent domain and the grant of public lands in order to make it possible for the railroads to move west. But, aside from such incursions on behalf of the creation of a transportation and industrial plant, there was little if any active participation in the hundreds of thousands and millions of economic transactions that occurred in a growing and increasingly complicated society.

Individual Americans tended to regard their circumstances as dependent on their own industry and luck. Only in the extreme did families look to the community at large for assistance. And, in those cases where such assistance was necessary, it usually occasioned the burden of deep psychological wounds for the recipient. Self-reliance was almost a religious precept among our people.

Such an attitude was entirely appropriate to life on a continent in which natural resources seemed almost untouched. If a man and his family had bad luck in one place, they could with relative ease pick up and try another. The great migrations that settled the continent were made of millions of individuals who moved themselves and their belongings in search of a better life. Each of them had reason to believe, on the basis of the experience of those who went before, that such a better life might well be the result of starting over somewhere else in what seemed to be an endless tract of land and opportunity.

When the frontier closed at the end of the last century a new phase of America's economic development began. The industrialization of the continent now intensified. As the population grew, great transportation webs developed to supply it with an ever-increasing flow of goods and services.

The uncertainties of the business cycle gave pleasure and pain in turn. But they were regarded as no more controllable than the weather. There was little if any feeling among most Americans that government could or should do anything that would alter the ebb and flow of the economic tides.

In 1932 all that changed. In that year, and for much of the rest of the decade, 25 percent of working Americans were unemployed. That means that *one out of four* Americans was unable to support himself and his family by his own efforts. The Great Depression resulted in a sharply changed perception of what the government was obliged to do during economic crisis. Enormous upheaval occurred at a time when academic economists were taking a new look at debt and evolving new theories of how and when the public sector could exercise its influence in order to affect the economic climate. We ought to remember, too, that the great unemployment of the 1930's was accompanied by an equivalent deflation in the currency. In 1933, twenty-nine cents bought a 1928 dollar's worth of goods. That has been the experience through much of history. When economic forces are undistorted by outside influences, the inability of people to buy results in a reduction in the prices of goods and services. Depression and deflation have, historically, been part and parcel of the same dismal package. Only in our time have we managed to combine recession with a skyrocketing inflation.

There was a general feeling in the early 1930's that unless some of these new economic theories were tried out the anguish of such large-scale unemployment and the resulting hunger among millions of Americans would result in political and social upheaval. The United States government entered the marketplace as an arbiter and regulator and paymaster on a scale never before dreamed of in this society. Even then, it should be remembered, the public debt rose to only $8 billion.

Relief programs (in the past these had been left to state and local communities), public works programs, price regulations aimed at *raising* prices, minimum wage requirements, and an explosion of federal agencies to enforce these and other economic decision-making, rapidly became a part of the American scene. Government was now an active partner in the nation's economic activity. It began to make decisions in a much larger social context than ever before. It began to subsidize economic activity that was regarded as socially *and politically* useful. It made determinations as to what companies could and should do in the course of everyday business activity. It granted new powers embodied in law to the labor union movement, and most important of all, it provided for unemployment insurance and pensions for the aged. These measures enhanced the power of the federal government as a factor in the lives of individual Americans in such a way as to have consequences that have altered the very nature of our individual attitudes, and the structure of our social and political institutions. The government had become an activist element in the lives of each of us. Harry Hopkins, one of FDR's most powerful aides, put it succinctly when he gave an inquisitive reporter his recipe for the New Deal's success. "Spend and spend. Elect and elect."

But the Depression had merely laid the foundation for the stunning explosion of economic interventionism that occurred under the lash of world war. From a period of dark unemployment and economic lassitude the economy suddenly pulsed with enormous activity that demanded the employment of every able-bodied citizen. The industrial base was expanded and revitalized, so that at war's end the economy was poised for a fresh burst of growth in order to satisfy the pent-up consumer demand that had been unsatisfied through four years of war.

This country came through depression and world war stronger than ever. We were the mightiest economic and military power in the world. Some writers were labeling the period to come as "the American Century." And the penetration of government into our everyday affairs was taken for granted. Without that government involvement during the Depression the national burden would have been unbearable; and in the crucible of war there is a natural tendency to rally behind the flag and to look to the country's leaders as the arbiters of individual destiny. World War II, the greatest conflict of arms in human history, was certainly no exception. Because it occurred in the immediate aftermath of massive federal intervention against the consequences of depression, it seemed all the more natural.

The American people now expected government as a matter of course to play the role it had assumed in response to emergency. President Roosevelt, toward the war's end, produced an "economic bill of rights" that included the right to a "useful and remunerative job." And the Employment Act of 1946 made it a matter of law that it was the government's responsibility to provide "full employment." Through the fifties and sixties the partnership between government and business, government and labor, government and the individual continued to grow. It did so, for much of that time, in a business atmosphere of prosperity and stability that many Americans believed was directly related to this increased federal involvement in economic activity.

But the truth was quite different. Measures appropriate to periods of emergency were beginning to have an insidious effect on economic growth and decision-making. The social attitudes that I call the "psychology of entitlement" began to take hold in all sectors of society. Individual well-being and never-ceasing progress toward higher and higher economic goals were beginning to be regarded as matters of right rather than as expressions of good fortune.

As a politician I share the view of those Americans who think that material progress is the driving force of our society. I believe with millions of others that government can and must do all in its power to achieve such progress. But I also believe that the events of recent years have demonstrated that the *effective use of that power is severely limited*; and that when it is exercised indiscriminately and in blunderbuss style the results are just the opposite of those intended. An OSHA regulation (OSHA stands for Occupational Safety Health Administration) that requires four exit signs in a one-room factory that has only one door is hardly helpful either to those working in the factory or those trying to get out the door. It is just that kind of government regulation that has had the cumulative effect of undermining the foundations of a stable economy. Of course foolish and excessive regulation is only a part of the reason for the rampant inflation we confront. But it is a significant part, and its role must be seriously examined if we are to understand what has happened to us.

The benefits of federal regulations are achieved at considerable cost. Whether we intend to protect the environment by tough requirements for clean air in the form of additions to automobile equipment, steel plants, and textile factories; or whether we intend to protect the consumer from shoddy goods when we impose regulations on the full range of activity under the aegis of the Federal Trade Commission, we are adding to the cost of products. Such a cost may sometimes be absolutely necessary. There is certainly very little sense in paying eighty-nine cents for a piece of tuna fish that will poison your central nervous system when you can save the agony by purchasing the same specimen for $1.25. But we must at long last recognize that we are paying more for the same goods in a regulated society than we would pay for them under a system with fewer constraints.

I believe there are answers to the cost-benefit problem and that we must put them into effect. But before we analyze what can be done to improve the way we make regulatory judgments let's examine some equally significant aspects of the system that have given us what seems to be perpetual inflation.

Government intervention across the board has done more to produce the number one problem our society faces than has any other factor. When we impose import quotas on foreign goods in order to play catch-up with inflation, when we raise subsidies, when we increase the minimum wage to a point where it no longer pays an employer to bring a young and inexperienced worker into his plant, we are creating a situation in which less will be produced and more will be paid in watered-down dollars and social stress.

8

All the King's Men

By virtually any yardstick, the performance of the U.S. economy in the 1970's was simply abysmal. It was our worst decade since the 1930's.

The most basic yardsticks of an economy's performance are the level and rate of growth of the standard of living of the population and the usual measure of the standard of living is average income per person. That standard is closely tied to the *real* gross national product, a measure of the total value of all goods and services provided in our society, adjusted for inflation, per person. From 1947 to 1973, real GNP per capita grew at 2.4 percent per year. *At such a rate each successive generation would be approximately twice as wealthy over its lifetime as the generation which preceded it.* But since 1976 our real GNP has slowed and fallen. The other usual measure of economic well-being, real disposable personal income, income after taxes, followed a similar pattern; it grew at about 2.5 percent per year for 1947 through 1973 and only at about half that rate ever since. But the storm signals are out. Such measures dramatically *understate the decline* in our economic performance for the period.

The post-World War II baby-boom generation moving

into the labor force in unprecedented numbers and the enormous increase of married women in the labor force leave us today with the *largest ratio of workers to total population in U.S. history*. That means that even though we have many more workers than ever before, our gross national product per person has been growing very slowly. We first stood still and then slipped back in comparison to our own history and relative to France, Germany, Japan, and other advanced economies. Some of them are growing three times as fast as we are.

No single person is fully responsible for the economic tides but the simple fact is that *President Carter and his advisers did not adequately account for the huge increase in the number of young workers and married women entering and reentering the labor force in analyzing the economic situation when they took office*. While the unemployment rate was still very high, most economists expected it to come down naturally. Carter's misjudgment set off a massive increase in government spending and public service jobs in order to quickly reduce the measured unemployment rate. If the administration had exercised restraint the unemployment rate today would have lowered to around 6 percent. Instead we paid a terrible price for thirties-style intervention in the mid-1970's. The Carter administration's quick-on-the-trigger spending stimulated a huge increase in the rate of inflation.

So deep is the wound of the Great Depression that the mere mention of the word "unemployment" conjures up in most people's minds the images of the breadline and the apple seller. But since World War II the unemployment rate has exceeded 6 percent only five times. In the last several years the average duration of unemployment has been three to four months; that is, once a person becomes unemployed he finds, on average, another job in fewer than four months. Coverage under unemployment insurance has been expanded to over 80 percent of the labor force; in 1947 only slightly over one half of the labor force was covered. Until government-induced inflation forced the recession of 1979 and early 1980 most recent unemployment was due either to entry or reentry into the labor force, persons quitting their jobs, and persons being placed on *temporary* furlough from their firms because of seasonal factors. That is, most unemployment was not involuntary unemployment due to an insufficient demand for labor in our economy. We have also more or less kept the full devastation of unemployment under control and have provided substantial income security to those who have lost their jobs. But as the proportion of unemployment due to long-term layoffs rises during the worsening recession, we must see the facts as they are, and take charge of our destiny.

Mr. Carter's abdication of economic leadership intensifies the recession triggered by his inflationary policies. Longer-term layoffs steadily rise and we must solve at the same time the substantial problem of structural unemployment of minorities, women, and teen-agers. Each of these groups has much higher unemployment rates than working white males. The unemployment rate for minority teen-agers has been about 35 percent or more for many years. That social dynamite must be defused by revitalized economic policy-making that will bolster our past achievements.

We Americans can take considerable pride in those accomplishments. We have gone a long way toward reducing poverty in what is by any standards a good society. For some reason it's unpopular to look at the facts and say we're on the right track. But that's what the numbers do say!

In 1962 the official poverty index revealed 22 percent of Americans living in families below the poverty line. In the next fifteen years that percentage was cut roughly in half. But even that official estimate is now badly out of date and seriously biased. It doesn't take into account the enormous growth of "in-kind" government transfer payment programs: transfers of goods such as subsidized housing, medical care, and food stamps. These programs either did not exist or were very small in 1962, so they were not included in the official definition of income. That is, *the official statistics include only cash income.* Any reasonable attempt to incorporate the value of subsidized housing, medical care, and food into the income of poor persons would yield a percentage of the population *below the poverty line of slightly under 5 percent.* It's not more pleasant for the 5 percent of the people who are poor than it would be for 50 percent. And we have to continue to make the efforts necessary to relieve the plight of those at the bottom of the income pile. But at the same time, let's recognize the staggering fact that we have largely eliminated poverty in the United States and that official statistics obscure the reality.

Another set of rather remarkable changes in the post-World War II labor force has been the explosion in earlier retirement, the decline in the average workweek, and the changing age structure of our population and labor force. In 1980 only one in five men over sixty-five is still in the labor force. In 1948 the number was about one in two. More people now claim their first Social Security benefit at age sixty-two than at age sixty-five and the average workweek has declined in the same interval from slightly over forty hours per week to about thirty-six hours. Simultaneously, there has been a big increase in the life expectancy of the elderly. These two factors—earlier retirement and longer life expectancy—combine to increase the average length of the retirement period by an astounding 30 percent. That means that older Americans need a much greater level of resources at retirement to finance the same annual level of income for longer retirement lives.

This longer retirement period will eventually combine with a startling increase in the ratio of retirees to workers in our society. The post-World War II baby boom plus the recent drop in the birth rate (even if the number of births returns to normal levels for the balance of this century) imply that the ratio of retirees to workers in our economy will increase by about 70 percent shortly after the turn of the century. We can expect enormous pressure on our fiscal and social service institutions. The best estimate of the trustees of the Social Security Administration is that the current ratio of one retiree for every three and one-quarter workers will increase to approximately one retiree for every two workers. We have to begin to plan for the graying of America.

In the 1980s aging Americans will comprise 16.5 percent of the population. That growth will expand in numbers and strength of influence into the closing years of the century. Yesterday's baby boom is well along life's road to senior citizenship. When so many of us become senior citizens, a transformed society will look at itself in a very different fashion.

Today's youth market, if the projections are accurate, will shrink and new markets for the aging will move into the forefront. The nature of our manufacturing and our industry and our advertising will appear very strange indeed to the Rip Van Winkle who went to sleep in 1979. You can be sure that the political process will itself yield the first signs of the new day dawning for older people. In the 1980s the needs and wants of older Americans will assume a priority afforded in a democracy to those who make themselves heard at the polls.

That is a prospect that reminds me of the time my cousin and I returned home from World War II and joined the American Legion. At the first meeting we attended one of the older members rose and made a motion to pay last month's bills. My cousin immediately got up and made his own motion to "beat 'em out of the money we owe." That's a motion we're not about to offer when it comes to paying up our obligations to retired Americans.

The foundations of the Social Security system must be strengthened because the contract we have made with future retirees must be honored. Productivity's expansion is necessary not just for a greater gross national product, but in order to supply the increasingly large share of that product to which senior citizens will lay justified claim. Stable currency is the answer to this problem as it is to so many others.

There is no greater problem facing the U.S. economy than gradually getting our inflation under control and restoring real economic growth to its historical level. In the two decades from 1947 to 1967, the inflation rate averaged only 1.6 percent per year. In the next decade, from 1967 to 1977, the inflation rate averaged 7 percent. By the time President Ford left office in 1976 he had brought it down to 4.8 percent; but after three years of Jimmy Carter's political economics we are blessed with an inflation of over 13 percent a year. This compares to inflation rates in 1978 of 4 percent in Japan, 3 percent in Germany, 9 percent in France, and 9 percent in the United Kingdom.

This kind of inflation, threatening to destroy the social fabric, is damaging for a large number of reasons. The most important of these is that it affects the incentive to save and invest. As the inflation rate rises uncertainty about the rate of return on investment also rises substantially. And in times of inflation investors are shy of risk. In many cases inflation has so distorted the rate of return after taxes that investors literally lose money on a pre-tax paper gain. A system that produces that kind of Humpty Dumpty action has seriously retarded saving and investment in the United States. In the late 1970's it was the king's men, themselves, who gave us an inflation that causes a kind of income redistribution gone mad. Commodities which are consumed disproportionately by certain groups in the population have greater rates of price increase than other goods.

For example, an elderly couple retiring in 1976 on a specific annual benefit from accumulated savings and pension would have seen almost 20 percent of the purchasing power of their retirement nest egg eaten away by the increase in the inflation rate since President Ford left office. If current inflation rates continue for the remainder of this administration, and another one, such an elderly couple will helplessly watch as between one third and one half of the purchasing power of their assets are wiped out by the increase in the inflation rate!

Perhaps the worst part of riotous inflation is that in addition to energy, the prices that have gone up most rapidly in the last decade have been those for food and medical care, the necessities of life that take most of the income of the poor and elderly. The awful paradox is that many of the government spending programs designed to help these people have contributed to the inflation that harms them so much, and we have to understand the causes of inflation if we're going to cure it.

Even after we account for the indirect pass-through of oil-price increases among other commodities, *energy price increases account for only 3 percent of our 13+ percent inflation rate.* If OPEC didn't exist we would still be running an inflation rate of 10 or 11 percent. Americans can't and won't put up with such inflation rates for a substantial length of time. The fever has already severely damaged the economy and deeply hurt millions of people.

The Carter administration's budgets have been so imprudent as to basically abdicate the role of fiscal policy in fighting inflation and to place us in a situation where we are relying virtually exclusively on the "independent" Federal Reserve Board to attempt to combat inflation. It's highly unlikely that this approach, without an intelligent tax policy formulated by an elected President and Congress will work for long. It also means that particular sectors of the economy, such as housing, automobiles, and consumer durables, will be hit much harder because of the necessity of a credit crunch than they would have been had a more balanced approach been followed.

For four years we have seen a succession of public relations gimmicks substituted for anti-inflation policy.

The President's first pronouncements offered voluntary wage and price "guidelines," cosmetic deregulation, and promotion of competition; reduced federal spending relative to GNP and corresponding reduction in the deficit; slower wage growth for federal employees, and "real wage insurance." What anti-inflation progress did we make from those exhortations? *A rise from 4.6 percent inflation to 13 percent plus in the first three years of his administration!* In the war against inflation, it's simply foolish to expect voluntary or compulsory guidelines to have significant and positive results.

The best evidence—provided by a liberal Keynesian economist—suggests that the Nixon administration controls, once removed, led to an inflation rate 1.5 percentage points higher than we otherwise would have had. Guidelines have led to excessive costs and unfounded expectations that fly in the face of budgetary and monetary policy realities.

Political pressure to impose compulsory wage and price controls must also be resisted. Controls produce shortages, service delays, quality deterioration, black markets, and substantial administrative costs for both government and private enterprise. Except during periods of extreme patriotic feeling and hardship, such as World War II, they have never worked very well. The need for restored economic and social growth demands that we provide a climate in which Americans will no longer fear that saving will turn their funds into Monopoly money.

9

Regulation + Taxation = Inflation + Stagnation

The form and ownership of capital is the lifeblood of this society. As savings and investment rates have declined, due mostly to inflation and heavy taxation of income from capital, our productivity growth has slowed dramatically. And recently we've had no productivity growth at all. We hear that most capital ownership comes from inheritance and that the distribution of wealth is extremly unequal in the United States. That is, at best, statistical sleight of hand. Government capital and the capital owned by the nonprofit sector are a much greater proportion of capital in the United States than they were a half century ago. That means that the share of total capital in the United States owned by individuals has been declining rapidly. Labor's share of national income has risen enormously: wages and fringe benefits now account for about 80 percent of the gross national product whereas they accounted for less than two thirds as recently as the late 1950's. Some reliable economists suggest that about 80 percent of the total capital owned in the United States belongs to people who have accumulated savings over their lifetimes rather than from inheritance! In addition to that, pension funds and other types of group savings have spread capital ownership to the general public as never before. Pension funds own approximately a quarter of the value of shares on the New York Stock Exchange. Workers old enough to have accumulated a substantial stake in a pension have as much to gain in an increased rate of return on the capital owned by their pension as on increased wages for the remainder of their working life.

In 1968, Otto Sik, who was Alexander Dubcek's finance minister during the Czech revolt against their Communist masters, suggested that Czech workers be given 10 percent of the capital in their ostensibly socialist firms. Several weeks later the Russians invaded Czechslovakia. In the meantime, American workers have continued to secure an ever-increasing piece of the capital action in the United States. That achievement has been endangered by the recent plunge in saving and investment that has been matched by an abysmal international economic performance on the part of the United States.

We engineered an enormous expansion of world trade in the last decade and a half but our share of world manufacturing exports declined from *29 percent in 1958 to 19 percent in 1978.* While we've been running enormous trade deficits, other advanced countries which rely still more heavily, relatively, on imported oil than do we, such as Germany and Japan, export more manufactured goods than they import, thereby running a trade surplus (about $20 billion each in 1978 for Japan and Germany). Obviously, as the domestic value of the dollar has fallen rapidly, and as our inflation has gotten worse relative to that in Western Europe and Japan, the average value of the dollar versus other currencies has fallen as well. Expanding our exports would do much to cure our trade balance, employment problems, and inflation. We must look to government to do its share because nowhere has the change in the American economy been more evident than in the growth of government spending and in taxes.

A half century ago, in 1929, only 10 percent of the GNP

passed through the public sector; today that figure exceeds one third. Government spending is about 37 percent of the GNP. In 1929 only a quarter of the then much smaller absolute and relative amounts of government spending was done at the federal level. Today well over two thirds of it is done at the federal level.

Just as government spending has grown substantially and the level at which it is spent has shifted from the state and local government sectors to the federal government, so the composition of federal government spending has been drastically altered in recent years. In 1952 transfer payments accounted for only 15 percent of the then much smaller absolute and relative amounts of federal government spending. Today 53 percent of total federal spending is on transfer payments to individual citizens. So enormous has been the growth of transfer payments that they now account for 14 percent of personal income (as opposed to 2 percent in 1929). This includes programs like unemployment insurance, welfare, Medicare, Social Security, food stamps, housing allowances, and many others.

Obviously, the growth of transfer payment programs has been one of the major reasons for the reduction of poverty in the United States. Much of this is socially useful, but even in Keynesian theory, government spending stimulates the economy when the spending is on goods and services, not when it is on transfer payments. Government must begin again to encourage growth and not just redistribution of a static income.

As government spending has grown in the last century, so have taxes grown. The major change is the enormous increase in the relative importance of Social Security taxes in the last twenty years or so. Social Security taxes are now the major source of tax burden for a majority of American families. They are the second largest item on the federal budget and are gaining rapidly on income taxes. Further, while we have largely gotten people who earn low incomes out of paying personal income taxes, and reduced the tax rates on the very rich in the personal income tax, the rapid increase of government spending and inflation now leave us in a situation where high tax rates are no longer the exclusive right of the rich. The median earner faces a combination of federal and state income taxes, payroll taxes, and other taxes which exceed 40 percent on *additional* earnings. That is, the high tax drag on the incentives to work, save, and invest has spread to the general population.

The rapid increase in government regulation has had large, not fully understood effects on our economy. Some of them are necessary and others should simply be thrown into the great federal shredder in the sky. First, there is the traditional regulation of a variety of industries such as transportation and public utilities. The reasons for such regulation are generally well founded—decreasing cost may make pure competition unfeasible and some form of regulation and fair rate of return the only acceptable alternative to dealing with what might otherwise be a "natural monopoly." A second type of regulation involves intervention in sectors of the economy where there is a substantial national interest and public concern over the private sector's performance. One of the worst examples of ineffective regulation is the government's performance in the energy industry. While rapid changes in energy prices, and a variety of other factors such as defense concerns over the proliferation of nuclear material, are sufficient cause for grave concern, our current practices for the most part can be seen as a second-rate parody of a central planning bureau in the Soviet Union.

Controls on energy prices have retarded exploration and production, created shortages, and caused so much uncertainty about future availability as to create a more chaotic situation in the energy sector than would occur without substantial government intervention.

The policy of our government should be to decontrol the

price of oil and gas as quickly as possible, to get out of the fuel allocation business, to stop wrapping every oil well in government red tape—and then to dismantle the Department of Energy.

Even as we conserve energy we must make it possible to discover new fossil fuels on our own territory and to develop alternative sources in the years ahead. Pilot projects for such development, combined with a windfall tax that will put those profits back into energy, research, and development, are among the first steps on the road ahead.

I'm convinced that the TVA provides a model for many of our future energy projects. The government tests them, spins the viable possibilities off to the private sector, and maintains supervision over small installations that will measure cost effectiveness against the new energy supplied by private industry.

The new "social regulation," especially in the areas of pollution abatement and safety, has both costs and benefits. It is difficult to measure the impact of these regulations on the production of cleaner air and water and greater health, but my own experiences tell me that we are getting more of these nontraditional commodities today than we did a decade ago. It is also clear that we are paying a price for them; that substantial pressure is being placed on individuals and firms to adjust technology and living styles much more rapidly than can be done efficiently. What is absolutely inexcusable in the behavior of the social bureaucrats is the propensity to ignore totally the cost of compliance and the economic harm done by too much regulation. Compliance cost is very often a large multiple of what government itself spends in regulating the activity. A good example of this is Senator Edward Kennedy's National Health Insurance Bill. While he estimates the "cost" of his National Health Insurance Bill at about $45 billion, this is only the direct cost to the federal government. That particular bill also requires an enormous expansion of employer contributions for medical insurance. But the Kennedy estimates do not include these costs in the total cost of the legislation.

"Off-budget" government activity is another inflationary balloon. To the estimated $30 billion deficit for fiscal 1980 on the books, we must add an estimated $12 billion deficit for "off the books" government economic activity.

There are a substantial number of quasi-government agencies whose activities are not included in the official budget. For example, the Federal Financing Bank will run a substantial deficit in 1980. The total estimated federal deficit off the books is about 40 percent of the on-the-books deficit.

The combination of slower real economic growth, high inflation, high and rising taxes, increased privately mandated activity, and declining international competitiveness have joined with the extraordinary changes in the population of the eighties to create an enormous and justified discontent with government spending and budget policy.

Some people have argued that the unhappiness with government is like the hula hoop and will soon fade away, that it is largely the aftermath of Watergate and related activities. Nothing could be further from the truth. The discontent with government spending and budget policy is deeply rooted in the economic problems of the last decade.

After two and one half decades of steady economic growth, the typical tax-paying working family has seen no gain in their standard of living in the last half-dozen years. Their earnings have barely kept pace with inflation and rising taxes, and *what little real economic growth there has been has gone into increased transfer payments which the working tax-paying population does not receive.*

Our major long-term economic problems have shifted from unemployment and insufficient spending to high inflation, sluggish growth, inefficient government spending, and adverse private incentives. If government has come to be viewed as the savior of the ordinary person against the ravages of unemployment and the destitution of poverty, people now have the right to expect that the government policies that have done much to mitigate unemployment and reduce poverty will be made more cost effective.

It's time to tighten up. The rapid growth of government spending, government deficits, and the raging inflation they have induced have seriously impaired our ability to provide a steadily rising standard of living for working Americans, and it is clear that a growing percentage of American people now *blames the government* for these economic ills, just as it once thanked the government for serving as a buffer against unemployment and poverty. People won't stop blaming the government until government gets off their backs. By 1978 a majority of the voting-age population of the United States, born since the Depression, had personally experienced high taxes, inflation, and sluggish growth as their major economic problems. The discontent with overgovernment and overregulation is likely to increase as the years go by unless the political community begins to respond in ways that work. What must be done?

10

What Must Be Done

The major goal of government spending over the next decade should be to try and make our current spending programs more cost effective, to provide for moderate expansion of our best existing programs and a few new ones where the need is clearly evident, and to get rid of those programs which are not cost effective. Stabilizing the share of government spending in the gross national product as a target would not shut down the public sector; it would not only permit an expansion of current programs at the rate of inflation, but would allow a modest development of new programs as real GNP grows. The rate of growth of government spending must be reduced so that the private economy will have the scope to produce increased goods and services; to provide an environment in which cost effectiveness is properly rewarded within the public sector; and *to make it possible over the next four years to cut taxes permanently and substantially.*

The way to put productivity and investment back into the economic mainstream is to put the American people's money back into their own pockets. A targeted tax reduction will enable investors to invest, savers to save, and capital formation—the machinery and equipment needed to improve productivity—to increase at a rapid and substantial pace. This

101

is a four-year plan for private enterprise and against public boondoggle.

What this country also needs is not a five-cent cigar but the facts about the way government spends its money. I intend to see to it that Congress considers a "Truth in Budget" act, legislation intended to put before the public all of the facts about what's coming into the treasury and what's going out. It's hard to believe but there is no one place where a citizen or a congressman can find the complete story of the cost of those "off budget" items and the dollars spent on regulatory activity. At the very least we should require our elected representatives to be fully aware of what the budget really is.

The people who are ready to pay for *their* programs with *your* taxes must be made to understand that tax revenues rise about one and one half times as fast as *nominal* income. When the GNP goes up 15 percent, 13 percent due to inflation and 2 percent due to real income growth, tax revenues will jump 22 percent. That is both stupid and unfair tax policy. When we finally stabilize the share that the government spends of GNP, the federal treasury will have, for the first time in years, an extra 7 percent of tax revenue to reduce the deficit and reduce taxes.

The next President must act on the economic facts. It is imperative that we reform the tax system to remove the disincentives which have been created and expanded to cover most working Americans during the last ten years. Our current system of personal and corporate taxation severely retards the incentive to save and invest. That's why I believe that in addition to a targeted tax cut, we must seriously consider a long-term switch from corporate and personal income taxes to a personal expenditure tax.

Such a change could be the driving force in a successful effort to restore saving and investment as the healthy foundation of a strong American economy! If we should take this path we must be careful to protect older Americans who have reached the point where it is necessary and useful to the economy to spend the funds they have saved for the retirement years. Others, too, must be protected from any sudden, severe change in direction. That's why I believe the next President, Congress, and the American people should begin a great debate that would ultimately lead to a more equitable and sensible tax system than the collection machine that now threatens the future. Discussion of the merits and possible flaws in moving toward such a system must be fully examined over the years.

We might, as a beginning, consider a universal IRA account in which anyone can make a deposit for retirement; currently, such accounts are limited to those people with self-employment income or who work in a firm which does not have its own pension plan. But, many workers, particularly younger workers, move around from firm to firm and don't become fully vested in a pension program until very late in life. Such a universal IRA account would enable them to save for their own retirement without the penalty of double taxation of their savings. We could also consider gradual development and expansion of an exemption for interest income taxation. The major problem with most such proposals is that, in order to keep the government's loss to a modest level, they have very limited application. Under such plans most interest income will accrue to the well-to-do. As a matter of principle I believe they should apply to all who choose to save. The long-term investment return will give the government its so-called lost revenues and more.

The next President must encourage and work with the Federal Reserve to achieve a slower and more predictable rate of monetary expansion. The Federal Reserve in the last decade was usually forced to expand the money supply very rapidly and "legitimize" the inflation implicit in federal government deficits, and the Carter administration has now abdicated the fight against inflation exclusively to the Federal Reserve System.

The next President must himself present and fight for *a*

sensible budgetary policy, with a slower rate of growth of government spending, which will enable us to balance the budget in a year or two, and then to keep a balanced budget or run a surplus while reducing taxes. A slower and more predictable rate of monetary expansion will both add to economic stability and the ability of the private sector to forecast the future of the economy. It would also enable us to fight inflation without such excessively high interest rates and the harm they do to housing and the manufacturing of durable goods.

Government spending must also reflect increased government commitment to research and development. The share of government spending on research and development has fallen markedly in the last fifteen years. We need to increase such expenditures, as well as private research and development spending, in order to update technology and increase and modernize our capital stock. It is mandatory for government to enable American entrepreneurs to compete effectively in world markets—*and to improve our technological capacity for defense.*

We have generated a complex series of regulatory reforms and new social regulations, and their full economic impact had not been forecast. These policies are adding substantially to costs, uncertainty about the future returns to investment, and creating a variety of other untoward economic effects. Some of them are also producing important social benefits.

I've spent many a day weighing the costs and benefits of reduced pollution and increased safety; my personal experience convinces me that a comprehensive review and rationalization of regulatory policy is essential. The best way to do this is not to create new boards of regulators to oversee the current ones; as I noted earlier that's the job of the congressional oversight committees.

The congressional committee system can really work wonders; it's a training ground for government. The closest parallel I've ever seen to it is trying a lawsuit as a young lawyer and watching more mature hands at work in the court-room. You learn by osmosis as you watch and follow by example. It's not a conscious process, but that's the way it happens.

The same sort of thing occurs in committee hearings. You watch the technique of older members, people like John Sherman Cooper, Caleb Boggs of Delaware, Ed Muskie, Jennings Randolph, and you begin to get the feel for asking the probing-type questions (without committing yourself to a point of view) that produce a variety of answers. That really is the essence of oversight and of legislative skill. It also produces some terribly, terribly boring hearings.

Just as the junior members are destined to have the last draw on seats in the Senate chamber, the junior members are the ones who conduct those laborious hearings. I would sit there for day after day after day listening to the most incredibly soporific testimony on the most esoteric subjects. Finally, though, I came away from it knowing I knew more about this particular subject than just about anybody living! To this day I retain a detailed knowledge of the catalytic converter, air-quality standards, the interstate highway system, the ABCD road system, federal aid to states, and other areas I do my best to forget. The congressional committee system is composed of good, solid, *elected* talent.

A new President must press the button of cooperation and join with those committees to see to it that appropriate utility studies are done. We should then make the current set of regulatory agencies more cost effective where socially desirable and eliminate the rest. *We simply need to get rid of the false notion that because a market may not work absolutely perfectly in some circumstances the government will automatically do better.* Too much experience proves the opposite. A less than perfect free market may well be better than a less than perfect government regulatory system!

International economic policy must be totally overhauled to restore the promotion of U.S. exports and a sensible trade balance to its central position in maintaining economic health both at home and overseas. We have almost totally ignored the possibility of removing the United States trade imbalance by expanding exports. We have focused almost entirely on curtailing imports of foreign oil. It is certainly desirable to curtail energy imports, especially when alternative sources of energy that are not too much more expensive may be found. But we shouldn't use the energy crisis as whipping boy for our export failures. Many other countries much more dependent on foreign imports of oil than we are run trade surpluses with an aggressive promotion of exports.

Our antitrust policy needs careful reexamination. Many believe that it now inhibits the role American firms could play in the world economy. While other countries' governments often arrange for several firms within their respective countries to unite to promote their competitiveness vis-à-vis the rest of the world, we would arrest American executives if they tried to do so. What was appropriate in 1890 may no longer be realistic as we enter the 1980's.

We need to recognize that our problems of competition are more international than domestic; and that promoting the U.S. in world trade will benefit all of our citizens. A variety of tax and regulatory reforms should be considered for the promotion of American interests abroad. The U.S. economy has changed rapidly in the last decade or two. And social and political policy must at long last be responsive to that change.

I believe in growth. Settling for what we have condemns the poor to enduring poverty and condemns the nation to stagnation and eventual decay. The federal government has been discouraging, even punishing, growth for a long time, and we have come to our present state of economic distress as a direct result of that misdirected policy.

A government that takes between $100 and $200 billion out of the economy every year to satisfy its appetite for regulation is a government that has grown fat and lazy and too big for its own good.

I believe we have been eating our seed corn for too long, that we need to encourage more savings, more capital formation, more investment in the future and less consumption in the present.

To do that, we need to change a punitive tax code which increasingly reflects a sinister view that profit is an evil thing. Profit is not evil. Growth is not evil. And the sooner the political leadership of this country begins to reward rather than to punish profit and growth, the better off our country will be.

Unless our current trend is reversed, we will all be the poorer for it, but especially the poor. Inflation hits them hardest of all, and the social services on which they depend cannot be provided by a bankrupt nation. Wealth which has not been created cannot be shared.

If America's economic strength declines, our role as a world leader will diminish as well. A country whose economy claims a smaller and smaller share of the world marketplace, whose standard of living is surpassed by one global competitor after another, is a nation in decline—a follower, not a leader.

If the United States is ever perceived in these terms, not only the economic but the international political ramifications will be staggering.

The time has come to turn the tide. The time has come for the United States of America to get down to business.

We have no providential right to preeminence in this world. Our ancestors worked to establish it, and we must work to maintain it.

The problems of the American economy affect the rich and the poor, the worker and the unemployed. When we solve them, and we will, the problem of unemployment will disappear and the funds for adequate social programing will be available. The ability of minorities, women, and poor people to move toward the goals they have a right to reach will be enhanced in a climate of stable growth. Any other kind of climate will assure us only of social tension and the possibility of bitter divisions that would make the 1960's look like a lodge picnic. There is no margin for error.

Part III
Saving the Social Contract

11

Civil Rights and Back Channels

In 1966 I came to Washington as a freshman senator from Tennessee. I was uniquely situated, although I had no idea of what was to come, to participate in and observe one of the major transitions in the history of the American system.

Lyndon Johnson was a powerful presence in the White House. The Vietnamese War was about to reach peak combat intensity. My father-in-law, Everett Dirksen, was the leader of the Republicans in the Senate. And, "the Great Society" was the slogan of the day.

Looking back, I can see that those first years in Washington for Howard Baker were really the end of a long period of government by coalition. New elements in the way we govern ourselves were about to be unveiled. The old dominance of the process by the formal institutions of the presidency, Congress, and the courts were about to be challenged in an unparalleled way. A kind of direct democracy was beginning to confront the institutions of representative democracy and we have yet to see the final results.

As a congressional brat and later as a young lawyer I spent considerable time in the capital. Only two years before my own election to the Senate I watched Senator Dirksen negotiate with President Johnson on a continuing basis in order

111

to get the Civil Rights Acts of 1964 and 1968 through the Senate. That was no picnic. A Democratic President, confronted with deep and historic splits in his own party, needed the votes of large numbers of Republican senators in order to achieve the passage of breakthrough civil rights legislation.

Whatever his faults, Lyndon Johnson was a man who knew how to deal with people one-on-one; and so was Everett McKinley Dirksen. Many was the afternoon the President would quietly slip into the Republican leader's office to discuss the best way to handle the legislative battle that was about to erupt on the Senate floor.

I remember one time before I was elected to the Senate, I had come to Washington on business. Having a couple of hours to spare before getting the plane back to Knoxville, I dropped in on Dirksen's office to spend some time with him. I just enjoyed being with Ev. He gave a spice to life that I think I appreciate even more now than I did at that time.

It was about six in the evening when Dirksen's long-time secretary, Glee Gohien, came into the office to say that the President was on the phone. When Dirksen picked up the phone his mellifluous tone was very formal. "Good evening, Mr. President." He stood and strolled about the desk as the conversation continued. Gradually, the tone in the voice changed. It became personal, almost intimate. Finally, he said, "No, I can't come down to the White House after work." After a long pause: "Well, I can't. You recall I came down last night and I got home late and Louella was angry."

As a Tennessee country lawyer I was a little startled at the informality of this exchange with the President of the United States. He never called him Lyndon, he always called him Mr. President. But the warmth penetrated the formality. After the conversation ended Dirksen and I carried on a desultory chat as he finished off his desk work. Then, not more than twenty minutes later (a very short time when you consider it), there was a commotion in the front room, in the little reception room, and the door came open and the first thing I saw were two straining, flea-bitten beagle pups. My recollection is they were on a single leather leash and Lyndon Johnson was attached to the other end of it. And there was one Secret Service man literally stumbling, trying to keep in front of the President. There was a whole bevy of security people behind, trying to keep up. Johnson was a towering figure. And it was comical to see this huge figure, this long leather leash, these straining beagle pups, and these breathless Secret Service types trying to be protective of a man who looked as though he could take care of himself.

"Everett," said Lyndon Johnson, "if you won't come drink with me, I will come and drink with you." Without a word Dirksen got up from the desk. They went in the back room and opened a bottle of Jack Daniels whiskey. And there they sat, the two of them, Johnson talking and gesturing in that boisterous Texas style and Dirksen in his smooth, unctuous, almost Shakespearean manner. They stayed there chatting and I sat there sipping and listening for a good couple of hours. I missed my plane.

Everett Dirksen was a careful leader. He had to take measured steps if he was going to shepherd his Republican troops into the civil rights camp. There was a wide divergence of views among Republicans as well as Democrats as to exactly what the civil rights law should be and how far it should go. It took careful and artful egg-stepping to reach an accommodation that could satisfy all of the groups that finally comprised the substantial civil rights majority. The vestiges of century-old divisions had to be dealt with in order to achieve the legislative culmination of the civil rights revolution. We've had civil rights bills offered and passed in the years since. But the real struggle for governmental commitment to equality was waged and won during the period of the Johnson–Dirksen entente.

The civil rights laws of the sixties were among the most significant public policy decisions in American history. But their passage is notable for another reason, too.

People in every part of the country, under the pressure of their consciences and under the pressure of other Americans who simply refused any longer to continue to accept second-class citizenship, were beginning a long struggle to reach accommodation. The South of course was the heartland in which the struggle was waged. But even in that part of the country attitudes and emotions varied with the geography from county to county and from state to state.

I am a product of the "Mountain South," of the Cumberlands. That region of the country was pioneer, frontier country. It's where the colonists first came across the mountains. Tennessee was thought of as the West. Daniel Boone came through the Cumberland Gap, and it still has a frontier flavor. In a way, it's caught even today in the eddies of that influence.

The people who settled there did not become plantation owners. They became backwoods hunters and trappers. You couldn't grow cotton on the side of a mountain and there was game and forest in profusion. During the Civil War, partly because there were no cotton plantations and there were no slaves, the mountainous South stayed fiercely loyal to the Union.

Once I looked at a world almanac for 1868 which was reprinted by the publishers a century later; it was astonishing how the voting patterns from that time were the same as the voting patterns are to this day. Republicans do well in the same counties as they did then. The Civil War century has ended but that tradition continues. It's a tradition of Republicanism, of dedication to individual liberty, of frontier spirit, ruggedness.

In that region of the country, blacks simply weren't thought of as chattel possessions. That mountainous region of the South had its share of troubles and sit-ins during the fifties and sixties but it never had anything like the big cultural clashes that occurred in Mississippi and Alabama.

I was never obliged to go through a great conversion of political faith to the idea that blacks were entitled to participate as full citizens of the Republic. On the contrary, I remember the Fair Housing Act being referred to by its detractors as the open-housing bill. But it quickly dawned on me that if you're concerned about fair housing legislation the best way to test that theorem is to think of its antithesis. Are we going to have *closed* housing? Are we going to have *unfair* housing? Most of the civil rights issues were eventually resolved for many of us exactly on that basis.

That was the last time, to my knowledge, that effective coalitions *were marshaled within government itself* to achieve large aims on behalf of a growing national consensus. It was a prime and the most noble example of what John Calhoun called the doctrine of concurrent majorities. A multiplicity of groups and individuals with varying motives, and sometimes with clashing intentions, were enabled to achieve an overriding objective by using the tools afforded by representative government. The Constitution provided the framework and the men and women elected to public office expressed the national will.

The Constitution doesn't say anything about the back channels used by Lyndon Johnson and Ev Dirksen to get that civil rights legislation passed. It doesn't say anything about drinks with the minority leader, and passing the time of day over the phone. Nor does it say anything about casual invitations to the White House. But even though it's not written down anywhere a President who has a warm relationship with his colleagues is a long way toward getting his job done.

Jerry Ford had that talent. He truly likes people. He has a good intellect, he was a good student, and he grasped a subject well. But one of his greatest gifts is the ability to make people relax and feel at home. Maybe that came as a result of his years as minority leader in the House of Representatives. I remember when I was helping him in his campaign for nomination as President. One night we were at the White House planning a political event. I was there, Bob Dole was there, Bob Griffin was there, maybe some others. We were in the little office off the Oval Office, talking about politics. Ford buzzed up the butler—the White House has the most spectacular butlers in the world; they look like they've been there since George Washington. This fella was tall and angular. His uniform was a little threadbare, just enough to give it class. He had steel-gray hair and President Ford asked him to bring him a martini and he sort of swept his eye around the room and a couple of us said we'd join the President. It seemed like the cordial thing to do. And then another one. And just as we were leaving I said, "Mr. President, I may never be in this office but just in case I ever am, don't you let that man get away! He makes the best martini I ever tasted!"

Relaxation, a little laughter now and again, even some trade-offs and logrolling are all useful and legitimate parts of the political life. I remember as a small boy, that my seventh-grade civics teacher took a dim view of logrolling. That was something that was done in the bad old days when Alexander Hamilton and Thomas Jefferson were at each other's throats.

Washington, D.C., you know, is itself a product of logrolling. The northern states and the southern states had divergent interests during the colonial period that aroused mutual suspicion. The national capital was carved out of Virginia and Maryland only after a bargain was struck at a dinner attended by James Madison and Alexander Hamilton. Madison, representing the view of the southern states, was opposed to the new government's assuming the debts of the old colonies. The reason was that the northern colonies, much more heavily populated than the farming country of the South, were burdened by a much greater debt load. When Hamilton agreed to locating the new nation's capital in the South, Madison promised to get his southern colleagues to vote for the federal assumption of the debt. Thomas Jefferson, by the way, who was Hamilton's most vigorous political enemy, was responsible for setting up the dinner. Now that's logrolling!

I remember the expression of disapproval on my civics teacher's face when he passed along that information. I just know in my bones that other seventh-graders in other American schoolhouses were afflicted with the same conviction that compromise, deal-making, logrolling, or whatever else you want to call the politics of accommodation, were inherently evil. That misapprehension, rooted in good intentions, has resulted in widespread misunderstanding of how things can be achieved under the democratic process. It also reflects, I'm afraid, a misunderstanding of human nature.

The genius of our society has been its ability to assemble "concurrent majorities" on behalf of most of the legislation that has reflected national policy since the early days of the Republic.

The people you send to Washington are not saints. At least I haven't met any during my tenure here. You send them because you expect them to represent your attitudes and at the same time, hopefully, to have enough strength of character to vote their convictions on those occasions when they differ from yours. Of course, if that happens too frequently you won't send them back again. That's one of the risks of the game. Your representatives, in a sense, mirror their constituencies. They conduct the business of politics in much the same way as you conduct your own affairs. That means that they must many times compromise their views when it is necessary to achieve an important goal. "Give some 'n' get some," they say. That's why the Constitution has been such a marvelous instrument. It was designed to effect the politics of compromise. But in the late sixties and seventies a number of events occurred that have brought into question the way the process works. I believe we have yet to face up to the paramount issue of our time. How is our system to function in the light of those events and of factors that have never before been present in American life?

12

Vietnam, Vietnam

The Vietnamese War was the most destabilizing episode in our history since the Civil War. Its effects have reached far beyond its political consequences in terms of the balance of power or the question of victory or defeat. They have gone to the heart of the governing process itself. The shift in our policy in Vietnam took place in a dramatic context of events and pressures that almost made the institutions of government appear to be irrelevant.

Americans have been involved in great, difficult, and sometimes questionable conflicts before. The War Between the States was of course the greatest. Its psychological consequences still echo today. The war with Mexico was bitterly challenged in the House of Representatives and in the Senate even as it was being fought. (Abraham Lincoln, a member of the House from Illinois, failed to win reelection because of his bitter opposition to the Mexican war.) World War I, and World War II in particular, strained our resources to their capacity. In 1917 and 1918 there were outbreaks of violence against Americans of German extraction; and in the Second World War we literally interned American citizens of Japanese descent. As in the history of any great nation the American drama has been laced with individual suffering and group tragedy. Fortunately for us it

119

has also been a chronicle of unmatched human hope and fulfillment. But the explosion of twentieth-century technology has set us on a new and uncharted course. Its rewards have been staggering, and we have yet to tap the fullness of its possibilities. Those rewards carry with them new demands on our resourcefulness. That's particularly true in the case of government and its relationship to the people.

Most of us think of television first as a medium for entertainment, and second as a way to catch up on the news. In a single generation it has become much more than either. Since the days when Milton Berle's shadow first flickered across seven-inch screens in 170,000 living rooms across the entire country, the rich technology of instant communication, in full color, has made us more aware and more sophisticated than any civilization in history. Nothing comes without a price and the effects of television on the political process must be addressed if we are to understand much of what has happened in recent years, and if we are to make intelligent decisions as to how to deal with the problems we must solve now.

Fifty million Americans who are eligible to vote in the 1980 election were school children in the years when President Kennedy and Robert Kennedy and Martin Luther King were murdered in cold blood. Most of them saw those events played and replayed on television. Many of those same children moved from the schoolroom to the streets in order to protest the Vietnamese War in the late sixties and early seventies. The writer Michael Arlen called the Vietnam conflict "the living-room war." That simile was painfully accurate. For the first time in history Americans could eat dinner, look at television, and watch a war in which their sons and brothers were killing and being killed ten thousand miles away.

How could we think that a people, and particularly young people, would respond to the events of the sixties in any other way than they did? We no longer had a buffer between our individual selves and the reality of political violence and bloody warfare. It was no longer demanded of us that we color words like "battle"—"wound"—"refugee"—"murder"— "starving" with the product and quality of our imaginations. It was all there to see in living color. These acts of violence and the nightly panorama of human misery were placed in immediate visual proximity to the televised statements of congressmen, senators, and presidents, who at best could offer only tentative captions to onrushing events. The images and the bromides created deep and conflicting anger that unfolded its consequences in protest, riot, and death.

For nearly twelve years the nation's emotional circuits have been overloaded. We have been confronted with the painful actualities of conflict with which politics deals, and the politicians among us were no better prepared for living-room homicide and warfare than anyone else. Never before have we been so close to so many realities that have traditionally been so far removed from our everyday lives. For the first time in American history congressional legislation and presidential decision-making came to seem ancillary to the real action on a living-room screen.

We were responding directly to direct pressures as a result of information presented in the vivid and painful guise of immediacy. Lyndon Johnson's "abdication" would not have occurred only a few years earlier. The enormous fact of policy as response to the impact of picture was quickly absorbed by the full range of issue-oriented Americans.

The right to petition was now secondary to the privilege of time on the tube. Media events were no longer the exclusive bailiwick of political managers and candidates for public office. They became the device whereby anyone with a cause attempted to get the message across to millions of potential allies and adversaries.

In the 1980's television news reporters, news producers, documentary film-makers, and editors may well be the most significant element in the political process. If there is a fifth branch of government it is the communications networks. We have been administered a dose of culture shock that has never before been equaled in intensity and impact.

Technology has called its own constitutional convention. And the American people have inevitably ratified the decision. When political men and women develop the policies of the eighties full account must be taken of the new partner at the table. The partnership was first manifested in a sharp and public way when executive and congressional action responded to the direct intervention of hundreds of thousands of citizens in opposition to the continuation of the war in Vietnam.

The sharp split over that war came to vivid life on the nation's television screens every night of the week. Whether it was one of the many marches on Washington, the Chicago riot in 1968, the march of New York's hard hats in support of the war, public draft-card burnings, or, the most anguishing moment of all, the death of four students on the campus at Kent State, there was an urgent sense of the social fabric being torn to shreds. Many in Washington felt besieged by their own constituents.

That was the most difficult issue for me to reconcile, to metabolize. I have a deep and abiding conviction that when a national policy is established, that, except for extraordinary considerations, the country should follow that position in foreign policy. And I had supported President Johnson even though I had a nagging concern that we were in over our heads; and I was mindful of Ev Dirksen's remarks that Vietnam might very well be the undoing of Lyndon Johnson, as indeed it turned out to be. Dirksen was thinking as much about the cost of the war as he was about the social impact. That had not yet reached its full intensity before his death.

When Nixon came in I remember a gradual and increasing disappointment that he didn't liquidate it sooner. I guess I thought he might end it more or less as Eisenhower had ended the war in Korea. But I stayed with it, and supported him in spite of a growing unease. Nevertheless, my doubts and concerns about the handling of that episode were quickly submerged in my indignation at the painted faces, the vandalism, the Vietcong flags, and of some of those mass demonstrations.

I'll never forget the day that the Vietnam protestors said they were going to shut down Washington. I was determined that they weren't going to shut me out of the Capitol. One of my staff members came to my house in his car and we drove there together. We locked the door, started down the parkway and up Virginia Avenue. Just before we reached the circle near Kennedy Center a whole group of protestors rolled barrels and oil drums in front of us. They were all painted up. They dragged bus benches and the like in front of the car. Ron and I looked at each other, I nodded, and he floor-boarded that car and drove right through them. We sent oil barrels flinging in all directions and bus benches splintering into the air, but we got through and went on to the Capitol. I felt drained and unhappy, but I was determined that that group was not going to shut me out of fulfilling the lawful functions of government. I think that the national psyche was affected somewhat the same way.

We all had a gnawing fear, even an emerging certainty, that this had gone on too long and in the wrong way; but there was a growing indignation, an anger at the nature of the antiwar protest that was going on around the country, the bombings, the kidnappings, the terrorists, the oil barrels, and the like. It was a great relief to me when that began to subside and it was over. But it would be foolish for me or anyone else to deny that the decisions which culminated in American withdrawal from the Vietnamese War were a direct result of the impassioned and highly visible protests of at least half the population. Those passions and that protest were fueled by the almost personal exposure to war forced by the television age.

13

Watergate and the Wired World

The civil rights revolution of the sixties was the first major event, in a sense, to foreshadow the enormous effects of television on the political process. Martin Luther King's leading the march on Selma and telling millions of Americans "I have a dream" is one of the most important parts of this country's folklore of heroism. One must wonder whether Dr. King's energizing personality would have achieved such immediate success without the new instrument of instant communication. It took Ghandi, with whom Martin Luther King has been compared, fifty years and a world war in order to achieve his objective of an independent India. But the surge of civil rights activism culminated in startling success in less than a decade.

The implications of that victory and the intense involvement of millions of Americans in the process that ended the war in Vietnam signifies a new age in American politics. Constituent demand and government response are much more closely linked in time than ever before. Government is monitored in far greater detail than was the case in the pretelevision age. It goes without saying that there are great advantages to this new situation. Government can never again be what it was before electronic communication wired the world for sight as well as sound. The insulation of most people from national and global events is no longer possible. I remember when I was a boy going to see the movie *Sergeant York*, with Gary Cooper. I particularly enjoyed that film because it was about a hero from my own part of the country. A few years ago I happened to catch it again on one of the late-night television shows, and I noticed something that hadn't made an impression when I first saw *Sergeant York*. The picture captured the flavor of a mountain community completely cut off from events that were about to change the lives of most of its people. Gary Cooper was genuinely unable to understand why he was expected to go and register for the draft in order to fight in a war against people he didn't even know existed.

Much of the film's tension and most of its effectiveness were related to the slow and gradual involvement of Sergeant York in the ambience of the world war. He was, at first, bewildered, a stranger in the world. He was almost literally sucked into the vortex of great events. There was something bizarre as well as touching about ceremonies in which York was decorated with the nation's highest military honor. There was nothing strange about a Tennessee country boy who knew how to shoot, who knew how to fight, and who knew how to lead men. Those qualities can emerge anyplace in any person. But in 1940 it was still possible for a film to comment on the strangeness of uprooting a mountain man and placing him on a field where a French general would kiss him on both cheeks.

Even though it's fast disappearing, there's still a vestige of that isolation in some parts of the Tennessee mountain country. Something happened to me not too long ago that illustrates the point rather well. I've always been a great admirer of Cordell Hull, who served as secretary of state for most of Franklin Roosevelt's presidency. I'm sure my admiration rose at least in part because Cordell Hull came from my part of the mountain. He was born and raised two counties over from where I live in Tennessee. One weekend, two summers ago, I was driving back and forth through that region taking pictures. I saw an old country store, and there was a sign on the side of the wall that said, "Hull's Store." It was sort of a picturesque place, and it was in Cordell Hull country, so I went inside. Nobody knew me, or at least nobody showed any signs of recognition. A group of men were, literally, sitting around a potbelly stove in the summertime. They were sitting around there "spittin' an' whittlin'," as they say. I walked over and asked, "Is the Hull Store, like it says on the sign out front, related in any way to Cordell Hull?"

They sort of went into their burrow and put their heads down and chatted together for a few minutes. Finally one of them popped up and said, "Is that the one that went off to Washington?"

That placed a different perspective on being secretary of state.

For most of us in 1980 that sense of strangeness is no longer present. Every moment of our lives, in one way or another, we are reminded that we are very much a part of a world in which we feel at home even though the chances are that we'll see most of it only on our television screens.

Some of you remember the weekly newsreels that were shown in the local movie house. It was the high point of the week to spend Saturday afternoon at the show. And the newsreel was as much a part of the show as was Buster Crabbe playing Flash Gordon. It was a community experience, a kind of "gee-whiz . . . look at that" experience. And the reality it communicated was relieved and erased because of the infrequency with which we went to the movies. A week's interval broke any connection we might have made with the fragment of reality momentarily caught on the screen.

Before television came to play such a large role in our lives most Americans relied on newspapers, magazines, and books to tell them about the world outside job and family life. The printed page offered time for reflection, rereading, and, occasionally, reassessment of one's views. There was a tentative quality about our responses to the events that made the headlines. People generally were inclined to defer to the authority of those who knew better. Today, if the polls are at all accurate, that deference is very much a thing of the past. The multimedia exposure, to which all of us have sometimes unwilling access, has also made each one of us an expert. The power of the visual image is unmatched in its effect on human attitudes and behavior. In the last twenty years we have been subject to such a variety of those images that many psychologists believe they have shaped a new kind of individual character and formulated new social relationships. As a politician I'm particularly interested in how those relationships contribute to the way in which we govern ourselves, and to the kind of political change they imply.

I remember a *Life* cover picture by Margaret Bourke-White in the late 1930's. A mother, kneeling on a railroad track in devastated China, wept as she cradled a dead child in her arms. That searing picture symbolized for many in my generation the horror of war and the tragedy of uprooted lives. It made Chiang Kai-shek a hero in the United States and helped to shape much of the political action of the late thirties and early forties.

But that photograph was a unique event in 1938. Its intensified equivalent is now a nightly experience in almost every home in America. We simply can't know the full effects that this kind of connection with immense, continuing human tragedy has on us as individuals. But the political implications are already beginning to appear. If people can't be isolated from events, government can't be isolated from people. Elected representatives were once the only filters for the thoughts and feelings of their constituents. "Back home, they say . . ." and people would nod with interest. But now all of us are drawn tightly together; the governed and the governors are no longer separated by distance or time.

The Watergate hearings were as powerful a demonstration of television's impact as one could ask. I was an active participant in those hearings, and as painful as they were to me because of my position as ranking Republican member, I can't help but feel that they signified a basic and lasting change in the relationship between the governors and the governed. My own involvement was so significant that I think a personal digression is in order.

For me those hearings were the most pressure-filled and stressful days of my public or professional life, and there was tension enough for a lifetime. I was, after all, a loyalist. In 1968 I thought Richard Nixon should be the presidential nominee. I worked for him. I campaigned for him, I did television commercials for him; and I celebrated his victories with him. In 1972 the election campaign was more or less routine as far as I was concerned. I never had the slightest doubt that the Watergate story was completely without substance. I was certain in my own mind that nothing would come of it. Then Hugh Scott, who was minority leader at the time, called me without warning or prior consultation and asked me if I would be the ranking Republican on the committee. I had no serious thought that I would; for that matter I had not thought of the Watergate Committee or the Presidential Campaign Investigation Committee as being a serious undertaking. Scott and I had run against each other for the Republican leadership, and some people thought this was "Scott's revenge"; other people said it was a Scott gesture of reconciliation, but in any case we met in the back office of his suite and I agreed to serve on the committee as the ranking Republican.

At the first organizational meeting with Sam Ervin and the other members, Ervin immediately made the suggestion that the committee be arranged with a chairman and vice-chairman instead of a chairman and a ranking member. That was a significant difference, because the vice-chairman, under the Senate rules, usually has a different set of authorities and powers than a ranking member does. He can sign subpoenas, he has his own staff, and he can authorize travel and expenses. He presides in the chairman's absence, which is not ordinarily the case. But Sam Ervin was determined that this would be a completely bipartisan effort.

I grasped that as an important development although I didn't realize until later just how important that was. It also created a rapport between us. I did not know Ervin well at that point. I knew him as a colleague, and I'd watch him perform on the floor and I respected his position. Ev Dirksen had once told me that he was a great constitutional lawyer. Until Watergate I had always wondered why Dirksen thought that, because I'd seen no particular evidence of it. At the time, of course, I was a fairly young and highly critical lawyer. It became very clear, very quickly that Sam Ervin had special talents, and that he was a warm human being. His allocation of resources and staff was also a rather generous gesture.

I have to confess that I really thought of the Watergate Committee as the Democrats' best effort to put a different face on a bad defeat. They had been overwhelmed, and the Watergate break-in was all that they had left. I thought the inquiry was going to make a minor story and a little splash, and give the Democrats something to talk about in 1976.

Shortly after I was asked by Hugh Scott to take on the assignment, I told my administrative assistant, Hugh Branson, that I would like to speak to the President privately about the hearings. I had made up my mind that I wanted to tell him, as senior Republican member of the committee, that nobody was going to hassle him. But I also wanted him to know that I was disturbed by what I was reading in the papers about the President planning to refuse to permit his staff to testify on grounds of executive privilege. When I got there, and I met with the President in the Executive Office Building, I began the conversation by saying, "Mr. President, I want you to know I'm your friend." I mentioned the fact that he'd been through the political wars for me at his own expense when I ran in '66. I told him that I thought this was a political exercise that we had to go through because of grumblings about the huge defeat of the Democratic party in 1972. But, I went on to say, "There's enough lawyer left in me to presume to advise you on how you ought to do this; and what I think you ought to do is send your major witnesses up there, pounding on the door, and demanding to testify." I recall commenting, "If they can't tell your story better than a collateral and secondary witness, you're in real trouble. But in any event, as a lawyer, I recommend that you get off this executive privilege and separation of power stuff and send them on up there." Nixon's voice dropped, and that was the first moment when the thought flicked across my mind that there might be more to this than political harassment. He looked gray and tense. He would not agree to send his people up. He talked around the point.

I was startled enough to say, "I assume that everybody's all right in this thing; and I worry particularly about my old friend John Mitchell." I knew John Mitchell before he came to the Hill. I used to practice law and he was sometimes counsel on the same matter. Nixon got very gray at that point and said, "Well, John may have some problems."

That was the moment I knew what we had on our hands, although I didn't know the details. It was also the moment when I changed my attitude toward the whole Watergate issue.

Thinking back on it, I later realized that there was a taping system and that's why Nixon lowered his voice. I didn't lower my voice. I kept booming out at him. But *his* voice was low and gravelly.

I left the Executive Office Building very shaken. And I came back and puzzled on what had happened. I never talked to a soul about that meeting. I puzzled on it for a day or two, and I finally came to the conclusion that I had no alternative in deference to my own integrity, to my responsibility on the committee and my heavy responsibility to the party, because by then I could see the rocks ahead. I made the statement "I'm going to follow the facts wherever they lead me."

All sorts of speculative stories have been written, some that purport to be factual, claiming that there was a back channel of communication between the White House staff and my staff or between Nixon and me. I never had a suggestion from the White House from Mitchell, from Nixon, from Haldeman, from Ehrlichman, from Dean, from anybody.

It was a lonely and difficult situation. I was the senior Republican, with the President, in effect, under indictment. And though I was a lawyer to my marrow, I was a lawyer without a client.

I was at a cocktail party one night at which a large number of friends of the White House were present. The atmosphere was frigid and I felt most uncomfortable, something like a man without a country. It went on like that for some time. But it had to be that way. I believe the committee bipartisan approach left the Republican party fit to fight on another day.

I had, after meeting with the President, the feeling that the Watergate scandal could cause the greatest setback in history to Republican fortunes. I could almost feel the waves pounding against the party that was part and parcel of my life. In some moments of really severe depression I anticipated its destruction and I was determined to do everything I could to see to it that the Republican party would not disappear because of the abuse of a few individuals in high places.

A new kind of personal accountability had come into being. For days, millions of Americans watched intently as the most powerful figures in the land attempted to justify their actions as public officials. It was my job as committee member to assess for myself what these actions had been, what they implied, and what their consequences should be. But, and this was the awesome thing about the Watergate hearings, we committee members were only a fraction of the jury. We wrote a report, but the American people were able to come to their own conclusions on the very same evidence and the very same images that were offered to the investigation committee. It was a dramatic illustration of how rapidly the role differences between politicians and voters have faded.

14

Prime Time, Direct Mail, and Single Issues

Most people have other things on their minds than the workings of government. That's one of the principal reasons why representative democracy has been so successful. It may not be politic to say so but a dash of public indifference is sometimes useful to the efficient workings of the government machinery. That's because the heat of debate occasionally blows out the lights.

There is, however, a new breed. A significant number of the people who care deeply about questions of public policy have learned the lessons of the sixties and seventies. The great dramas of civil rights protest and Vietnam divisions played out on television have intensified the effectiveness of smaller groups who wish to bring their concerns to public attention. When these groups come to Washington, or gather in one of the other great cities, they are far more interested in appearing on television than they are in delivering a message to the City Council, the Congress, or the President of the United States. Television has demonstrated its ability to satisfy these appetites for group expression. And as a result American politics is in the midst of a sea change. We still live under the old social contract but some new clauses have been slipped in that deserve careful study.

Single issues in the United States have usually been re-solved in the context of bargaining one advantage for another and accommodating to some extent a different point of view in order to achieve at least a portion of your own objectives. But the immediacy of communication in our time has made single-issue politics a much different game. Groups tend to organize themselves on an "all or nothing" basis. There is a dangerous tendency to attribute evil motivations to those on the opposite side of the question.

Most of us are aware of what can happen when individuals insist on the primacy of their own rights and privileges. In industry it's called "going by the rule book." Subways don't run on time, airline passengers are put on three-hour holds ten thousand feet in the air, cars don't move off the assembly line; civilization's amenities and necessities can no longer be taken for granted. Tension replaces ease in the way people go about their everyday lives.

The brokering of these legitimate separate and special interests is one of the government's most important func-tions. Special interests, as noted earlier, are universal; and the intensity with which we pursue them has a large effect on the rate of progress of the human race. But the "me first" attitude has recently begun to have subtle and insidi-ous effects.

The abomination of American politics is the high-pressure use of direct mail to raise funds or to foster special interests. I would like to abolish that kind of direct mail but it would be unconstitutional. I think it is the bane of political life, and I despise it. I think it has a distorting effect and it has produced the single-issue special-interest lobbies that we now find roaring through the corridors of the Capitol in Washington and in every legislature throughout the country. Some of them have good purposes, but they are at variance with the idea of a broad-based political system based on national and state parties that appeal to a diversity of broad-based interests. Just as the newspapers during William Randolph Hearst's time manipulated the policies of the country, radio had a similar effect in Franklin Roosevelt's time, and television jolted us in the fifties and sixties, so now direct mail has tapped the potential for inflammatory rhetoric. It stimulates fads and prejudice. In politics it almost never appeals to the more generous aspects of humankind. Its increasing misuse endangers free government. Many issues are capable of rousing large constituencies to express themselves in no uncertain terms.

I happen to come from a part of the country where gun-control legislation is anathema. Not surprisingly, I share the view of my constituents who believe in the constitutional right to bear arms. It is an issue on which feelings run high on both sides of the question and these people don't hesitate to let politicians know where they stand.

The question of the "right to life" or the "right of choice" relates of course to abortion, a subject freighted with all of the moral, cultural, and religious weight a single issue can bear. The Supreme Court's decision to permit abortion has moved the question out of the courts into the mainstream of intense and frequently bitter public debate. Here, too, advocates of choice and those who oppose abortion in any form have concentrated their efforts in an attempt to defeat those who either disagree with them or stand on some middle ground.

The Equal Rights Amendment is still another of the single-issue lightning rods. For seven years the question of whether to ratify a constitutional amendment mandating full rights for women has been before the states. The battle has been waged on grounds ranging from questions of serious substance to whether an amendment would require the abolition of rest rooms discriminating on behalf of one or another of the sexes. Here, too, "Are you with us or are you agin us?" is the single issue when election day rolls around.

When I'm asked why I voted against the time extension for consideration of ERA I point out that I voted for the amendment, but that I thought that extension by simple resolution adopted by a majority vote was simply extra-constitutional. The Constitution is to be changed only in a very particular and specific way, with a two-thirds concurring majority in both Houses of Congress and ratification by three-fourths of the states. I believe that constitutional rule should apply to every material aspect of the procedure, and that an extension of a period of years beyond that should be done in the same way, regardless of my commitment to the substance of the amendment. But ERA, like so many other emotional issues, takes on overtones and connotations beyond that which logic would ordinarily supply. My answer frequently does not completely satisfy the people who ask it, and they suggest by innuendo or directly that I don't believe in equal rights for women, or women's full participation in the public life of our country, and variations on that theme. I say, "Look, if the women in my life were any stronger the world couldn't stand 'em! My grandmother was elected sheriff, my mother served in Congress, my wife is on the board of trustees of Bradley University, Mount Vernon College, and Knoxville College; my daughter was president of the student body in her college. In my family we *live* equal rights for women."

Because there is such an energy and a dedication to equal rights and because so many women have tied it so closely to the Equal Rights Amendment, I think they run the risk of prejudice or jeopardy to the further extension of opportunities or the opening up of new possibilities. People on both sides of the issue are well organized. Their anger quotient, the energy that legislators find in their questions, or their responses, their boos and their cheers are somewhat troubling. That's especially true when you think, as I do, that progress of women in America's life is inevitable and inexorable.

I believe opportunities will continue to expand in the development of societal values on behalf of full equality of the sexes, and new concepts of education, of childrearing and family formation. It's just happening. That's the way it is, and that's the way it should be.

During my twelve years in the United States Senate I have earned a reputation for moderation. In today's political lexicon even moderation can be a bad word. In times past it may have seemed kind of dull. The implication was that a moderate person didn't have strong views, and didn't have much fun either. But the politics of high media intensity has changed all that. A moderate politician is even worse than a liberal politician or a conservative politician. There just doesn't seem to be much room left in the political arena for thoughtful evaluation of how to bring differing groups together and of how to accommodate their views in the governing process.

A good example of what I'm suggesting, and a painful example it is, was the fight over an appropriations bill during the Ninety-sixth Congress. The government of the United States nearly went out of business because the House and Senate couldn't agree on language relating to the expenditure of federal funds in cases where abortion is recommended by a physician in circumstances where the health of or life of a patient is substantially threatened. An amendment relating to the abortion issue had been tacked onto a bill appropriating money with which to pay the government's bills. Because of the dispute over the language in that amendment, federal workers went on half pay, Social Security checks were threatened, and only at the very last minute was chaos averted. This technique of provoking fiscal crisis is a form of government by coercion. It was first applied during the Vietnam days when "no money for the war" amendments were tacked onto one appropriations bill after another. Gradually the technique began to work. Congress literally cut off the funds that made it possible to continue to fight and the antiwar lobbies had scored their greatest victory. They also opened a Pandora's box, because today the practice of offering policy amendments on money bills threatens to immobilize government. People with strong convictions on one side of an issue can take exactly the same steps to make their views prevail as can their opponents.

I don't want to imply that all of this is brand new. Parliamentary maneuvering has always been very much a part of the political game. As a matter of fact, people from my own part of the country have well-earned reputations as masters of the art. Russell Long is one of the best examples I can think of. He, of course, is the sum total of his experience, and that experience extends back to his uncle Earl and his father and his mother. He's the only man in history whose mother and father both served in the Senate. He comes from Louisiana, which is a very special state in itself, and Russell is the composite of all those things.

Russell has one primary operating tactic, and he repeats it session after session and year after year. He simply saves the matter in which he is most interested until the last item on the legislative agenda and bucks it up against adjournment. Everyone wants to go home and that gives him enormous leverage. He did it in 1979 with the windfall profits tax. He's done it before with other tax bills, and he'll have the patience to do it as long as he sits in the Senate. I've come to think of the last month in the session as "the Russell Long session."

Unfortunately that kind of back-room maneuvering is no longer readily resolved by compromise. The issues themselves have almost literally been taken to the streets. Just think about some of the topics you've seen portrayed on television in the last several years; and just think about the style in which they've been presented.

Some years ago there was a poor people's march to the Capitol. We saw a mule, a coffin, hundreds of moving figures, and a series of thirty-second statements about the plight of the poor in America. Since then, we have of course seen passive resistance to the extension of nuclear power; that is, hundreds of kids and young people thrown into the paddy wagons and carried away to spend an hour or a night in jail. We've turned on the set to see farmers driving their tractors around Washington to let us know about the difficulties family farms confront in an era in which subsidies aren't keeping pace with the prices farmers must pay. We've watched mothers heap piles of roses as the symbol for the right to life in the waiting rooms of as yet unconvinced congressmen. That, too, has frequently been the setting for a fifteen-second episode of close-up, impassioned denunciation of abortion. We have seen pro- and anti-ERA women *and* men scream at each other in anger and even hatred. We have seen literally hundreds of thousands of people march on Washington in protest against the sometimes grotesque results of forced school busing. As they wend their way along Constitution Avenue they shout their messages to individual passers-by; but the television camera is the audience they seek for that quick fifteen-second exposition of the anti-busing position.

We see nationwide moratoriums on this or on that. We see young people blocking access to the New York Stock Exchange in order to prevent investment in nuclear energy. Colorful pictures, stimulating pictures, and then again a quick series of close-ups—this time of workers trying to get to their jobs in the Exchange. They, too, express themselves pungently and with considerable conviction. "Pigs, a bunch of animals, ignoramuses."

The language of debate has been coarsened beyond recognition. The heightened passion, encouraged by political fear, has changed the rules of the game in the halls of Congress and in the White House as well. But there is a stunning contradiction at work. For, rather than breakthroughs on behalf of one side or another in any of these emotion-laden issues, we have come to a point where it is almost impossible to achieve meaningful legislative progress. The penalties for disagreement with large and vocal constituencies have become so extreme that many senators and congressmen shrink from the very idea of compromise. This cuts against the grain of the parliamentary process and is in direct conflict with the constitutional tradition of two hundred years.

In 1978 and 1979 Congress organized special energy committees to negotiate differences on legislation needed to meet the energy crisis. Most of the members of those committees were highly skilled and knowledgeable legislative technicians. Many of them had a firm grasp of the issues and had specialized on energy matters for much of their political lives. But in the crunch they were unable to come up with bills that would satisfy at one and the same time the country's needs and contradictory demands of constituencies in conflict. Even now, stable and satisfactory priorities for energy action have yet to be established.

The separation of powers is a bedrock constitutional concept. Much less generally recognized is the *coordinate* function of the President (and the bureaucracy), the Congress, and the judiciary. If we're going to solve the problems of the 1980's this coordinate dimension of intragovernmental relationships must be emphasized as never before. We must end the government by stalemate that has recently evolved.

In the last three years a laundry list presidency has sent one bill after the other to Capitol Hill for congressional consideration. Rarely, if ever, has a proposed agenda been discussed in detail and in advance with the members of the key congressional committees that must give it consideration. On issue after issue the legislative process has stalled and on issue after issue presidential leadership fails. A sense of drift is exemplified by a legislative agenda that has no thematic consistency. There has been no attempt to move toward specific national goals. And, worst of all, there has been almost daily shift in emphasis in response to newspaper headlines and television news stories.

In one month we had a proposal to stimulate the economy by giving everybody fifty dollars. In a period of days a heavily publicized "reassessment" took place. The fifty-dollar rebate went down the tubes. The administration decided that unemployment alone was the nation's principal problem even as economists in the private and public sectors both pointed to inflation as a time bomb that could explode in immense social destruction. It was a signal that was obviously missed until much too late in the game. Coherent public policymaking has gone by the boards and we must take the necessary steps to restore it as the principal business of government.

15

What Must Be Done

In a time of political drift and economic uncertainty we may be on the eve of an age in which something very much like Athenian democracy can be restored. Twenty-five hundred years ago the citizens of Athens gathered together in the agora (the meeting place) and debated the public questions of their time. Every citizen voted on every major question of policy. It was government by referendum. In a republic in which millions of citizens span a continent such a system has not been possible nor may it be desirable. But certainly television and the new satellite and cable technologies on the eve of fruition make its electronic equivalent a likely aspect of the future.

We can respond to these immense changes in one of three ways. We can stick our heads into the sand and ignore the whole thing; we can attempt to dilute its consequences by political and social actions intended to link technical potential with political requirements; or we can recognize the wired world for the enormous opportunity it offers for expanding and improving the political process.

I believe that in the 1980's the President and Congress should take the initiative in seeing to it that the American people participate more fully in the day-to-day business of government. Inasmuch as television, even now, affords the opportunity to restore some if not all of the substance of direct democracy, legislation requiring the admission of television to all congressional debate in both Houses is a logical first step toward increased popular awareness of how the system works.

When the Foreign Relations Committee considers a treaty of great importance to the nation's future, when an Interior subcommittee marks up a bill that affects the water rights of millions of Americans living in the West, and when arguments are being made on how congressional elections should be financed, those hearings and those arguments should be recorded for television broadcast. A rapidly developing technology has made it possible to film these legislative activities without intrusiveness.

What could be more important to casting an intelligent and committed vote than seeing the way your representative handles himself in the Energy Committee hearing on how best to increase the production of oil and the effectiveness of the Energy Department's regulations on the allocation of heating fuel? Only a tradition locked to the customs of the past stands in the way of just such opportunities.

The House of Representatives must be given credit for taking the first tentative steps in the direction of regular "full disclosure." In 1978 the House installed television cameras, and the chamber's debates were recorded for whatever television stations and cable outlets wished to make of them. But the limitations placed on the way the cameras are arranged do more to distort the image of reality than to project it. Cameras must be focused directly on the chair of the speaker of the House and on whoever has the floor. As it is, the full flavor of the House in action, of people milling about, conferring with each other, calling out in response to the speaker of the House might as well not exist. In the fall of 1979 someone literally jumped from the visitors' gallery onto the floor of the House and the event wasn't even recorded because the rules prevented the cameras from moving!

I believe that both House and Senate must permit unrestricted television coverage of most congressional business. I hope that legislation will be introduced and passed to that effect in the near future. Such coverage of the SALT II Senate debate, when and if it occurs, would provide the American people with all of the information they need to assess the right or wrong of the Senate's decision. If we truly believe that an informed electorate is an essential national interest we have the means to achieve that end in a way we wouldn't even have imagined twenty years ago.

It is just as important that deliberations within the executive branch come under the lights. Let's say you're an optician in Sioux Falls, South Dakota; and let's say that the Federal Trade Commission has decided to make regulations about the prices you're permitted to charge for spectacles. Or let's say that the Environmental Protection Agency is considering new regulations on air-quality requirements in cities with populations over 250,000. Wouldn't it be a wise public policy for you to have immediate access to what is happening in those hearings? Wouldn't it be wise public policy for you and your colleagues, or for you and the other residents of your large city, to know which commissioners say what and why? Wouldn't you then be better able to make decisions as to how to respond to their actions? If the regulations implemented at these hearings are well founded and if they are widely disseminated they would probably rally wide public support. If there are substantive questions as to the wisdom of these regulations they would be more effectively challenged by citizens who know how they were developed.

It's a paradox of an age in which so much information is available to so many that there is a pervasive confusion about who does what in government.

A friend of mine was a candidate for the United States Senate in a large eastern state; and before he decided to run for reelection he took a poll to see where he stood with the voters. It was a representative group, unaware of the poll's sponsorship and ostensibly gathered to discuss some of the problems to which they thought government should address itself. During the discussion it became apparent that my friend, who had served in the Senate with great distinction for two terms, was being blamed for the absolutely dreadful record of garbage collection in the city in which the discussion was held. When it was pointed out that as a United States senator he had nothing to do with the garbage-collection situation, the general attitude was "Well, then he should make it his business."

I'm not under the misapprehension that Fred Silverman is going to film the nuts and bolts of day-by-day government for prime-time exposure on NBC. But I am under the distinct impression that such exposure is not the only or even the most desirable way for citizens to see the government in action. It seems to me that Congress should create a video bank in which all substantive administrative procedures and rulemaking sessions would be filed. Such a bank would distribute video cassettes of these governing sessions to professional associations and grassroots organizations that might find them useful. (I would also include those seventh-grade civics classes I mentioned earlier. The sooner students come into contact with the realities of the way government works, the better they will be able to affect its nature when their turn comes.)

Bringing the new electronic technologies into a direct partnership with the devices of self-government will be an ongoing process. There is simply no way to tell how satellites, cable, and the dozens of other variations on the communication theme will impact on the shape of America's long-term future. But even the first steps suggested here can play a significant role in bringing more and more people directly in touch with some of the forces that govern their lives. Those forces are personalized in the characters, and the interrelations, and the effectiveness of the representatives you send to the nation's Capitol. In the 1980's the President and the Congress will make every effort to reestablish a partnership for effective government.

Policy development and execution can best evolve in an atmosphere of close harmony. A presidential office in the Capitol is only the beginning of that kind of relationship. It seems to me that the President of the United States can best achieve his goals if he is in almost constant touch with the legislators who will eventually shape his program and pass it into law.

In today's world that constant dialogue can be effected when the President is in personal touch with committee chairmen and influential members of the committees that are concerned with what he regards as high-priority issues. We need leadership by example. I have the very simple view that different perspectives on law and on national policy can be reconciled when the people concerned have established close social connections. When the President of the United States regularly discusses the nuts and bolts of legislation over a lunch table he will have a serious effect on the way the process works. Occasional presidential indigestion and a congressional ulcer or two are small prices for putting efficiency back into the system.

Capitol Hill fairly swarms with representatives of the federal agencies who have an interest in the laws that are passed that affect their operations. Although this liaison activity is very helpful in most cases it is often not nearly enough to get the job done. People blame Frank Moore and his congressional liaison staff for the breakdown in communications between the President and Congress. I don't think they're any better or any worse than the congressional liaison always has been. The problem in this administration is with the President. Jimmy Carter, in my judgment, simply does not understand the leadership role of the President in respect to Congress. Lyndon Johnson understood. Jerry Ford understood it. A President has to know it intuitively. That doesn't mean having them down in alphabetical order to talk about thus and so. It just means calling somebody on the phone, or coming up to see them, or having them over for supper. It means knowing how to say "Look, we don't agree on this, but I've gotta have this one," and working it out. You can almost always work it out. Congress wants to help a President who leads!

In the 1980's we do need structural change as well as changes in personal relations. Just as the President should go to the Hill, Congress should go to the departments. That's why I suggest that there is a need for an ongoing congressional presence *on a consultative basis* in the principal agencies of the government. In the midst of the communications revolution there has been a breakdown in communications between the executive and legislative branches. Congressional oversight of the activities of the federal government, required by the Constitution, can be strengthened by an ongoing presence of congressional committee members and staff in agency offices. Such a system has its own risks. But under proper safeguards it would ensure a mutually productive relationship.

The adversary tone of congressional–presidential dialogue is a single aspect of a relatively new yet troubling situation. The ambience that has resulted from the decisions over Vietnam and the Watergate revelations has yet to be evaluated for its long-term effects on American society and political life.

During the Watergate period much of the press adopted the view that there is a natural adversary relationship between the United States government and the people and institutions who report on its activities. I find that conception disgraceful and dangerous. Webster's Dictionary says that "adversary" means "opponent; enemy." We've come to a pretty pass when members of the press regard themselves as the enemies of government. Even worse, the behavior of too many government officials has encouraged the media to adopt that view of the relationship. That has not always been the way the press regarded itself; and it has not been the way government saw or should see the press.

The gathering and dissemination of information about the way government works is just as important as the work itself. The monitoring of government activity is as important to the successful functioning of a democratic system as the governing process. In a sense it is very much a part of that process. As long as there is human weakness there will be the tendency to "accentuate the positive and eliminate the negative" by elected and appointed officials alike. Only an institution outside government control is equipped to call the shots accurately; and if the system is not to rot from the corruption of unaccountability a free, and even if occasionally irresponsible, press is necessary. But the role of the press also implies conscious membership in a society that holds basic values in common. Too often in recent years the tendency on the part of government to "manage" the news has engendered a corollary attitude by the press that under every rock there must rest a maggot of scandal. This subterranean warfare is the unhealthiest of all of the disputes that has burst out between various social and political groupings in recent years.

The press has the right and obligation to avoid reporting by government handout. At the same time it has the obligation to presume that the men and women who have been chosen to govern their country are as honest as the people they represent. The implications of a contrary attitude are so ominous that they don't bear scrutiny. The poisonous atmosphere in the political arena is in no small part the result of day-by-day reporting in such a way as to create the cumulative impression of malfeasance, hypocrisy, and dishonesty among public servants. The Watergate scandal and the enormous unhappiness with the Vietnamese War have engendered a mutual suspicion that has to be replaced by reasoned perspective.

It is obviously one of the legitimate functions of the government agency to present its decisions and activities in the best possible light. The people who make and implement decisions do so, with rare exceptions, because they believe that they are in the national interest. These bureaucrats, these congressmen, and senators, and even the President, may be wrong as often as they are right. Their actions must be subject to scrutiny by legitimate authority within the government itself and by the public through the press and whatever other devices spring from the grassroots. But confusion has been fostered between erroneous action and inadequate understanding, bungling and incompetence as compared with deliberate sharp dealing. That confusion has spread so far and threatens to become so deeply imbedded in the popular attitude toward government that it is much easier than in the past for the "no compromisers" to impose their views on reluctant public servants. When inherent respect for our institutions begins to crumble, moral fervor is too readily substituted for rational debate as the decisive factor in how and why we make decisions.

I believe that it's time for a recognition of what the stakes are when some of society's most influential sectors engage in an undeclared and unacknowledged war. The self-hatred that is manifested in much of the comment about America's role in the world, and about Big Business or Big Labor, simply does not represent the true picture of the way the tremendous majority of the American people feel about themselves and their country. The incessant self-criticism that dominates much of current social and political analysis will ultimately come home to roost in a paralysis of national will. The best prescription for a return to common sense in the way we treat our differences is complete candor by our governors as to what they're doing and why, access to the full record of government action and the background to that action, and a predisposition to believe that our fellow citizens are just as likely to have good intentions as not.

Perhaps only as time distances us from the impact of the early seventies can we reduce the burden of the distrust that impedes government's effective function. But we must at least acknowledge the problem if we are to solve it. For a politician it is no easy decision these days to challenge the press to match its demands for rectitude in others with an acknowledgment of its own equivalent responsibilities. Yet the truth simply must be confronted. Politics has become mean and nasty. If we don't find some way to recivilize politics in the United States nobody worth his salt is going to be willing to compete. Even more important, those who have the will to survive and win election to high office will find themselves unable to govern.

We need a new consensus of goodwill in the United States provoked and conditioned by our awareness that this country's margin for error is a thing of the past. The bewilderment of professional economists as to how to restore strength to the American dollar and higher productivity to the American work place is more than matched by government's failure to propose and win acceptance for programs and solutions dealing with those problems. The obsolescence of military equipment ordered and produced for the needs of the fifties and sixties is more than matched by the shattered morale of an intelligence community shaken by the public revelations of its methods and its failures. And the uncertainty in other parts of the world about American intentions and capacities is more than matched by a withdrawal of genuine commitment to the survival of friends and allies.

We must begin to take the actions that will enable Congress to make law, the President to administer the country's affairs, the economy to assert its strength, and American power to stand as willing surrogate for our friends and guarantor of our international interests.

Part IV

No Margin for Error: Americans Abroad

16

"Bearing Any Burden": From Munich to Saigon

The Strategic Arms Limitation Treaty negotiated by the Carter administration is at the center of the struggle over American foreign policy in the 1980's. In the process of that negotiation, in its results, and in the administration's attitude and actions in the struggle for its passage, the themes of the decline of American power and the erosion of determination to protect the national interest have been sewn into a tapestry of our government's self-deception and Soviet deceit. The SALT question and the results of the debate over its passage can best be described against the background of an American foreign policy that in recent years has descended into uncertainty of purpose and paralysis of will. It is a policy that has appeared to friends and enemies to lack focus or goals. The bipartisan foreign policy of World War II and the postwar era has been replaced by the rhetoric of human rights and the passivity of an unwilling actor on the world scene. In order to understand SALT we must first look at the results of a policy that has brought us to a point where it was negotiated and accepted by the President and his men. One can begin at almost any point on the globe where there is an American presence or an American interest. In most of these places such a presence or interest is "beleaguered."

Iran is perhaps the ultimate symbol of the decline of American power, and of the futility of United States foreign policy since the end of the Vietnamese War. The embassy tragedy is an extraordinary and painfully precise object lesson on the consequences of inaction fostered by fear. But it is only the most dramatic evidence yet offered of what is to be expected when a policy of drift is clothed in the rhetoric of human rights. How did a country that opened its national history with the vow of "millions for defense but not one cent in tribute" end the decade of the 1970's as helpless suppliant for the lives of our representatives abroad? Why have we come to be seen as helpless targets for the acts of vandals and terrorists, sometimes in the guise of statesmen, occasionally dressed as religious fanatics, but always contemptuous of American values and unafraid of American might? What has happened to "the leader of the Free World"? I take that phrase seriously. And, in 1980, it causes me to wince in embarrassment.

We were once prepared to lead; yet somehow our elected leaders have lost even the will to effectively exercise the obligation to defend ourselves against our declared enemies. If the days of the so-called cold war are over, our adversaries don't seem to know it. American interests are under fire in every part of the world and there is no coherent strategy either to protect them or to advance them. Our leaders seem to suffer the need to atone for actions in which most of them played no part; that means that they are accepting a burden of national guilt in your name and mine. But most of us find it perverse to weigh the contributions this country has made to the preservation of civilized values in the thirty years since World War II and turn them into a cause for self-flagellation and mea culpas. We expect our leaders to build on the foundations of yesterday's accomplishments in order to strengthen American aspirations for the future.

What are they apologizing for? Even more important, how are their apologies affecting the course of our history and the prospects that lie ahead for Western civilization? These are serious questions, and the answers must be weighed with care and acted on with determination. There is simply *no margin for error.*

Someone has to say it. We lost the war in Vietnam. That's it. We lost it. Our "withdrawal with honor," our "decent interval," never quite made it as the real thing.

We're a realistic and hardheaded people. A great many Americans thought Senator George Aiken had his head on right when he said "Let's declare victory and go home." Everyone knew what that meant. And at least it brought a chuckle. There was no laughter in negotiating for months on end about the shape of a table in Paris while Americans died in the jungle rot of Southeast Asia; and there was no laughter in watching our people make their hasty helicopter retreat from Saigon. No laughter and no little heartache at the sight of the allies we were forced to leave behind; and no laughter and much horror at what occurred when our *victorious*—yes, *victorious*—enemies occupied the territory we had given up. A presidential candidate in 1972 had called out "Come home, America." But in coming home as we did we left a not insignificant piece of our national pride in Saigon and Phnom Penh. And we must come to grips with that if we are going to reassert our strength and contend effectively with what we must do in the world of the 1980's.

The first thing to remember is that the war in Vietnam, no matter how it divided us, was an expression of the same purposes that had saved western Europe for thirty years from the kind of Soviet domination that has smothered human decency in the gulag of eastern Europe. Most Americans were with John F. Kennedy when he called on us to "Pay any price and bear any burden" so as to achieve liberty in the farthest reaches of the globe. They were with him, in part, because we had already begun to pay the price and to accept the leadership of that struggle from the moment we entered World War II. There was no one else to do the job, and the people of this country were not bashful about taking on the responsibility. And that's what the bipartisan foreign policy was all about. It was an expression of a period when a particular burden was accepted by all or most of us as the price of wealth, power, and liberty.

But times do change; a role that is appropriate to one set of circumstances does not necessarily apply in all. Our very successes in forestalling Soviet expansionism through the fifties and sixties raised questions as to an appropriate foreign policy in a world in which there appeared to be a new stability. That is one of the most fascinating aspects of the period in which we're living.

This surface stability in the relations between the Soviet world and our own emerged in the theater that had been for twenty years the principal arena of confrontation. That "relaxation of tension" in Europe was the product of deepening self-confidence on the part of the Common Market countries and a gradual erosion of the distrust that had plagued Franco–German relations for generations. It was furthered by the Soviet Union's awareness that the use of military force would be necessary if they wished to exercise dominion over Western and Central Europe. American power prevented that; and the starving peoples of postwar Europe turned into aggressive entrepreneurs who saw daily evidence that their system was infinitely superior to the fumbling Eastern giant in its inept efforts to provide minimal decencies for the millions of people it held under its thumb. Frenchmen and Germans, Italians and Belgians and Dutch were close observers of the rebellion in East Germany against their Communist masters; they saw the riots in Poznan in which one Polish Communist government fell only to be replaced by another. They observed the brutal repression of the Hungarian Revolution, and the Soviet invasion of Czechoslovakia under the rubric of "socialist solidarity."

It seemed to many in the West that the Russians had quite enough on their hands dealing with the recalcitrant population of their eastern "provinces." Although American leaders and their European partners continued to protest the need for vigilance and unity, a gradual erosion of the "ties that bind" was beginning to occur. People who were no longer worried about the bear's claws found the bonds of alliance constraining and even vexing.

The departure of France from the NATO Command was the first in a series of events that tended to put the NATO alliance onto the international back burner. An increasing tendency to sneer at Russian clumsiness relaxed fear of its intentions; those who continued to warn of its menace came to be regarded as Cassandras or, worse, as backward-looking bores. Similar attitudes found increasing expression in the United States even as more and more American troops were themselves engaged in the Vietnam War. The popular diversion of comparing this country's motivations in Vietnam with those of the Soviet Union in Eastern Europe found a ready reception among many influential opinion-makers. Some of the very same people who had built the architecture of postwar containment were puzzled, then angered and bewildered at our inability to win in Vietnam. For the first time since World War II the United States found itself in a position in which it could not dominate events in which it played a central role. It is an experience that has been too frequently repeated in the years since. That is the most important of the many reasons that we must reassess the way we make foreign policy, what its principal objectives must be, and how we can best achieve them in a world that seems to be going through an earthquake of change.

In earlier times the governors of the major powers could reflect at some length as to what the consequences would be if they embarked on a particular course of action. The time lag between decision and action in most cases vitiated the inclination to plunge into international hot water. The simple fact was that you couldn't get to any place in all that much of a hurry. Cool counsel frequently prevailed in such a climate of spaciousness. In our time, when the Ayatollah Khomeini's every glance was seen on three networks within minutes of its exposure to the camera lens, that kind of luxury is long gone. Tramping boots seem to march across continents in minutes, and naval guns fired in the China Sea are echoed in the world's chancelleries seconds later. Telephones are picked up quickly and words spoken calmly, hastily, angrily, intelligently, but always in the heat of action.

In such circumstances a change in the direction of foreign policy usually occurs almost unconsciously rather than as a matter of considered judgment as to its long-range implications. Since 1977 foreign policy has simply fractured as events crowded in, and decisions are most often made in response to the actions of others; the concept of a pattern of geopolitical action taken on the basis of long-range objectives is the exception here rather than the rule. I believe that whatever else may be said of Richard Nixon's shortcomings as President, he exercised statecraft in that traditional sense of a captain steering the ship of state to a particular destination. All of the postwar presidencies prior to his were dedicated to achieving goals determined by the Western Allies at the end of World War II and its immediate aftermath. The containment of the Soviet Union, the perception of a monolithic international communism were expressions of the needs and the judgments (some few were in error) of a generation ago.

In a sense John F. Kennedy was the last of the postwar Presidents. The Bay of Pigs debacle and the Cuban Missile Crisis were cold war confrontations brought to such heightened and fearful intensity that the fever broke, although the origins of many of the conflicts of our own day can be closely related to the climate of Kennedy's first years in office.

Kennedy's approach to these conflicts was conditioned by a sense of an American power that could not be matched let alone surpassed; if he walked the edge of the cliff, he did so in the full knowledge that the United States was bound to take action on the commitments made by a generation of Democratic and Republican Presidents; and he was sustained by the series of unbroken victories for that foreign policy whenever it was firmly invoked from the dark days after Pearl Harbor to the flight from Saigon.

When the United States found itself in a full-scale war in Vietnam most of the American people were bewildered by its sudden impact. It was a war that had slowly crept up to the front of the papers. For thirty years the Vietnamese had been fighting colonizers, occupiers, and themselves. For thirty years we had our hands full in other parts of the world. Southeast Asia was a concern, yes; but preserving Europe from Russian aggression came first. We sent our airplanes to break the Berlin blockade. We challenged the Soviet Union in Iran; and we won in the United Nations and we won on the ground. There was a civil war in Greece; there was the Marshall Plan. There was the threat of H-bombs and atom spies. There were political battles to keep Italy from going Communist and France from going Red. We repeatedly won these battles abroad; we won because our armed strength appeared to be invincible and because our economic aid triggered a European economic renaissance that ensured twenty years of prosperity.

Even as we had fought the Pacific war after the Germans were well on the road to defeat, the foreign policy-makers of the postwar era put Pacific and Asian concerns on the back burner. That didn't mean that there were no commitments. One President after the other did what he felt was necessary to preserve our Asian alliances and to fend off what was seen as Communist aggression. But the pot grew so slowly that in 1961 most Americans didn't know the difference between North and South Vietnam, Ho Chi Minh was just a funny name, and the names of our allies changed so fast there wasn't time to memorize them. Then, out of the blue (it appeared to most Americans), there were 500,000 GI's fighting in a jungle war that every General from Mac-Arthur to Ridgeway had warned against. It is easy to see in retrospect that we were in a no-win situation.

The Cuban Missile Crisis had seemed to put a period to confrontation; we were ready for a break in the cold war. But the heritage of leadership and obligation had an inertial quality. Policy-makers acted almost reflexively in relating the events of the past to newly realized dangers. When catch-words of the past like "Munich" were applied to a present that seemed to bear little resemblance to the world of forty years ago many Americans asked "What does Saigon have to do with Munich?" Our commitment to a less than vigorous ally gradually eroded. I believe strongly that today there is an uneasy feeling among many who came to oppose the Vietnamese War that, whether the conflict was right or wrong, the consequences of the events in the Munich of 1938 were not that far removed from the consequences of the events in Indochina in the mid-seventies.

17

The Iranian Mirror and Détente in Pinstripes

The American President and the American people, recognizing the foreign policy setbacks of the seventies, must forge a new foreign policy that reaffirms the preservation of national security as its principal aim. American commitment to serious alliances of mutual interest must be maintained wherever they are appropriate to the evolving nature of influence and power in the world. Much of that evolution is unfavorable to the American Republic and it has grown out of the climate of self-doubt that has dominated much of our foreign policy debate since war weariness ended this country's involvement in Vietnam. It is a self-doubt that is easily understood, but we can no longer afford it. Doubt of our capacity for action, uncertainty of the motivations of our leaders, and assuming a national guilt for napalm and death in Indochina have done nothing to alleviate the massacre our adversaries committed in Cambodia, have done nothing to prevent the forced migration of ethnic Chinese from their homes in Vietnam, and did nothing to alleviate the anguish of Tehran in 1979. It is time to recognize that where America overreached it did so in the cause of international justice; if some of our past allies had hands that were unclean by the standards of liberal democracy, their replacements have almost uniformly been bloody tyrants, whether they dressed as Muslim ayatollahs, or in the olive drab of Latin American dictators. The world of international policy is guided by the reality that not all people share our views of the sanctity of human life and human rights; and that alliance with the devil is sometimes necessary if the human endeavor is to continue at all. In 1940, Winston Churchill said just that when he extended the hand of alliance to the same Stalin who had murdered millions of his own people. In 1980, if we are to survive as a free society, we must once again recognize that hard truth. The threat to our survival is real. We have encouraged it by our actions of these last few years and we must redress the balance before it is too late.

As I write these words, it's the day before Thanksgiving in 1979. I'm sitting at the desk in my library at home in Huntsville, Tennessee, and the news of the death of a twenty-year-old American Marine in Islamabad, Pakistan, has just come in. The fate of the American hostages in Tehran is still in doubt and I've been on the phone with various officials in Washington all morning long.

It's a dark time. The apparent helplessness of the United States in the face of this kind of hostility has never been more bitterly demonstrated than during these last few weeks. There must be a change now in the way we look at the world, and in the way we deal with it.

I think that the Iranian thing has held up a mirror and we don't like what we see. I think that the disillusionment of Vietnam and the determination that we'll "never again" intervene in another conflict anywhere in the world has run its course. We Americans think of ourselves as a proud, strong nation. And if you withdraw from responsibility you're going to be seen as a nation in retreat. There's a fundamental tenet of the American personality that simply won't accept that. It goes all the way back to the frontiersmen when they first went across the Alleghenies and then trekked to the Midwest and across the plains to California. We've always thought of ourselves as independent, as strong, as a match for every challenge. This is the first period in many years when that has been seriously called into doubt. I don't know whether Jung was right about having a collective conscience or not. But I do know that there is an American personality and it doesn't like being second-best. It doesn't like being in retreat. It doesn't like being pushed around.

The Iranian Embassy is only three blocks from our home in Washington. On that Sunday, when they had their big demonstrations against Iran I couldn't resist the temptation. I drove down there and watched, and it was incredible. There they were, young men and women—in blue jeans and long hair—demonstrating just as their older brothers and sisters had demonstrated against the war in Vietnam. Their signs were demanding the most extraordinary actions against the Ayatullah Khomeini. The American flag was in such prominence and held in such respect that it dawned on me that a whole new generation has come home to the fundamental belief that America must be strong and outgoing. I think the transition from Saigon to Tehran ran faster than anybody would ever have thought possible.

The most serious error made by the foreign policy establishment in the years between World War II and the Vietnamese War, even until now, has been the tendency to apply our own standards of judgment to the perceptions and the responses of the leaders of the Soviet Union. Nothing has cost us more dearly than that truly irrational view of the processes of Soviet behavior.

It was easy to despise the evils of Stalinism. The stale and stilted vocabulary of Marxism–Leninism was applied to everything from biology to music; the failures of Soviet industry and agriculture were revealed in an outsize concern with security, and a megalomania rooted in the deepest kind of national paranoia and inferiority feelings. The horror of Stalinism, stripped of pretense by some of its own practitioners, turned out to be the horror of the grave.

A few of us even took comfort at Khrushchev's shoe-banging performance at the United Nations. For some, it was a sign of human feeling; for others it was the sign of the clown. In either case it relieved the image of monolithic Soviet strength. It was Khrushchev who gave us our first opportunity to misjudge the nature of a relentless adversary.

Fortunately, the Soviet Union does make large mistakes. It is not the inscrutable and unfathomable machine projected by the image of Stalin. If it were not for those mistakes Khrushchev's promise that our grandchildren would live under socialism might be more threatening than it now appears. But our consumer-oriented society is peculiarly vulnerable to packaging, and when I wrote about "surface stability" I meant it as the most serious example of appearance belying reality. When the gray garb of Stalin, and the almost jovial tantrums of the unpredictable Khrushchev were replaced by the blue pinstripes of Brezhnev, Kosygin, and company, too many of us began to think that we could do business with the Soviet Union in much the same way as we could deal with the chairman of General Motors or the president of the AFL–CIO. The Soviets, in a superb example of effective public relations, did everything they could to promote the deception.

Remember, the Brezhnev group took the helm in a direct response to two disasters for Soviet policy. One was the backdown at the height of the Soviet-engendered Cuban Missile Crisis; the other was the massive failure of Soviet agriculture that threatened famine in the early sixties. They adopted a "revisionist" approach to their dealings with the United States and it has worked just fine, thank you, ever since.

The summit meetings of the sixties (Johnson and Kosygin at Glassboro, New Jersey, followed by a host of others) had a much different flavor than the early gatherings during the height of the cold war. There was a genuine feeling among Americans that we could at last frolic with the Russian polar bear; we could deal with the Soviet Union in such a way as to reach accommodations of interest. And it was about time. World War II, Korea, cold war, and a deepening involvement in Vietnam were too full a plate for the American people to handle if there was a reasonable chance that our society was no longer threatened by nuclear extinction; that the U.S.S.R. was just another social system with a set of interests that were not necessarily antithetical to our own.

Americans are a peripatetic people, and we like movement in almost all areas of our lives. Certainly, there was a predisposition to search for the end of a period that had many of the trappings of the Thirty Years' War. I'm in no position to know the inner workings of the Kremlin, but I would be very much surprised if there weren't a considerable number of Soviet Americanologists who had similar attitudes. Nevertheless, the evidence of events and of our senses indicate that the men who call the shots in Moscow have never swerved from their ultimate goal of global political dominion. If they can woo American business into providing assistance to bolster their own inadequate resources and technology that is all to the good. The forging of those commercial ties has been one of the most effective weapons the U.S.S.R. has wielded in a conflict that for them has never been anything but one of the two central concerns of their foreign policy. The United States, in turn, sought its own advantage in bringing an end, or at least an armistice, to the adversary relationship with the U.S.S.R. In a society in which public opinion is by definition the ultimate arbiter of public policy it is difficult to maintain unrelenting preparation for possible international conflict and unswerving defense of interests that sometimes seem less than urgent. One of the principal elements of the democratic process is its reflection of popular demand. Government cannot long remain isolated from the moods and aspirations of the public it represents. Foreign policy and national security are, literally, in the hands of the people.

I know that some observers will scoff at the assertion; the war in Vietnam, the Pentagon Papers, and Watergate are for them the symbols of recalcitrant government blocking the people's will. The facts, however, are quite the reverse. The war in Vietnam had the full support of the American people for a considerable period of time, despite the emerging sense that we were sinking into an enormous rice paddy. The leak of secret documents during a period of war turned into an effective public relations weapon for the war's opponents, and Watergate set off a process in which the popular will was fully expressed within the bounds of constitutional law. Nothing could be more democratic than that.

A foreign policy expressing the popular will can be effective only when the majority of the people are fully aware of the complex realities of international relations. In the 1960's, and through the last decade, too many policy-makers, anxious to bring public opinion with them, found themselves instead following its tides.

The process was unconscious and unavoidable. But it had its price. For a war-weary people were all too ready to believe that we had achieved a just end to the war in Vietnam, that the Soviet Union was on the way to becoming a reasonable negotiating partner with whom lasting settlements could be made of outstanding differences between us; and that our long-time opponents wished only the achievement of a lasting peace based on a genuine balance of military and politica power between the two systems. Nothing could have been further from the truth.

Even as Secretary Kissinger attempted to establish "linkage" as an essential component of the détente for which every American wished, the Soviet Union continued to supply their ally in Hanoi with weaponry that encouraged them to delay a settlement for many months at the cost of thousands of Vietnamese and American lives. In the end, it was the same settlement that could have been reached almost a full year earlier. If anything should have signaled the United States that our foreign policy must continue, for the indefinite future, to have as its central concern the behavior and deployment of Soviet power, it should have been the intractable Soviet refusal to broker out the differences between Hanoi and a Washington anxious to leave the war on almost purely cosmetic terms.

We have refused to take Marxist–Leninists at their word, in much the same way as too many Americans and Europeans ignored the words in Hitler's *Mein Kampf* until he had written them again in the blood of millions. The Soviet Union is a state dedicated, in the words of its own testaments, to the extension of revolution throughout the world. The Marxist–Leninist dogma expresses, not succinctly but at great length, the view that capitalist–democracy will fall to the dictatorship of the proletariat. We must keep in mind that the Soviet state is itself an expression of that view, and that every action taken by the U.S.S.R. in its international relationships has been a demonstrable expression of Russian commitment to that end. As a result of that political commitment, two armed giants equipped for mutual destruction, and far worse, are in direct and long-term confrontation.

It is not easy to reduce these relations to their essential terms. But it is a necessity for public figures to openly express their recognition of facts that have been obscured by the passage of time. For if we have forgotten the immutable nature of Soviet ideology, the politburo has not. Soviet actions in recent years are revealing of a heightened confidence in their military power and the influence that Russian might wields in much of the world. It is a sobering record to review, particularly in the light of the slackening of our own efforts to project American influence beyond our borders, and of our hesitancy even in the councils of our allies.

It's time for a caveat and a paradox. We must continue to

extend ourselves in the attempt to negotiate meaningful agreements with the Soviet Union. There is no choice. The kind of world in which we live has produced a bizarre confrontation in which two irreconcilable opponents must do anything and everything to avoid a conflict that could destroy the earth. That single fact is the foundation of our hopes.

The United States is dedicated to the traditional precepts of foreign policy that have been accepted for centuries among the nations of the West and East alike. We wish to engage in international commerce with as much freedom as possible. Our citizens are to be permitted safe and reasonable access across borders and waters; we in turn protect the rights of others as they do the same. That is how we have historically defined American interests abroad, and our formal relations with other countries are structured to accommodate all of the mundane day-to-day activity that makes these things possible. Consular relations, exchange of diplomats, and a flow of communications between capitals are intended to assure just this kind of an international community. But the truth of the matter is that these foreign policy objectives are so broken by intermittent conflict that the failure of international comity is more often than not the subject of foreign policy and international relations. It is out of these breakdowns that what I call the "rules of repair" have evolved; and in the seventeenth, eighteenth, and nineteenth centuries, these repairs have been achieved through negotiations that struck a balance of power among the great nation states wherever they emerged as factors that had to be taken into account because of their power and their will to use it to satisfy their own ends. For the ineluctable truth is that international relationships are determined by various kinds of power. Ethical standards of behavior come into play as the expression of the civilizations from which they spring. But they survive as models for international conduct only if they are embedded in a society with the strength to act on behalf of its beliefs.

18

The Decline of the Western Will

At the end of World War II the carefully balanced structures of the past lay in ruins. For nearly thirty years the United States led the West in an unresolvable conflict with the Soviet Union. It was unresolvable because although our strength was supreme, our interests were the interests of individuals and groups of our citizens. As such they were varied, sometimes conflicting, and more often than not, they were compromisable. Our opponents were often inefficient. They sometimes blundered. They were certainly no match for our military power; but they intended to change that unhappy situation, and for at least seventeen years, since Soviet submarines sailed their missiles out of Havana Harbor (under the umbrella of observing American air power), that has been their single and unswerving objective. In early 1980 the U.S.S.R. is close to achieving that goal, and in 1980 our own leaders have difficulty in defining any national goal at all. But I believe that, unfortunately, the Russians have decided at least our short-term goal for us. We must maintain our parity and continue to match Russia's military strength if our institutions are to survive.

The days when foreign policy could concern itself primarily with freedom of movement and commerce are at an end for the rest of the century. The events that swirl around us raise fundamental questions about the literal survival of Western civilization. American foreign policy must deal with that issue first, or other problems will be for others to solve. The power of the weapons that have been dispersed among us, and the nature of some of the societies which have these weapons in their arsenal, erases all other questions from primary consideration.

Thirty years after the end of the war with Germany and Japan the maps of the world display totally new entities, and picture more dangerous instability. New relationships among nations are evolving even as these words are written, and the United States can help to determine their effects only if we make some changes of our own.

The Soviet Union and Eastern Europe still stand as one military entity with the Russians in complete and unquestioned command of the resources of power. But among its NATO allies American commitment to NATO's security has been privately, and infrequently in public, called into question by many of its military and political leaders. The NATO countries have tended in recent times to limit their association with the United States to questions of European security. There has been a steady erosion of direct NATO ties to American security concerns in other parts of the world; and, most damaging of all, some of the NATO allies have begun literally to war among themselves. When Greece and Turkey, out of an animus that goes back centuries, began to fire guns at each other, each of them threatened the United States with sanctions ranging from withdrawal from the North Atlantic Treaty Organization to raising the ante for the use of bases on their soil to forbidding this country the right to fly over their territory. There is something sadly askew when an alliance designed to protect the European states is used by some of its members to blackmail the principal guarantor of their security. We'll come to the SALT talks later, but perhaps the most vivid example of the decline of American power occurred when Turkey refused to permit us to monitor Russian compliance with its terms from Turkish territory or air space unless the Soviet Union *first granted its permission.*

We have found ourselves repeatedly in a situation where we negotiate among our allies for the permission to defend them. If, however, they no longer truly believe in our will to extend them our protection we have inadvertently given them some reason to think so. The uncertain path of American power in the world has caused unease, even among those who call themselves our friends. But, as in most cases, there are two sides to every coin. Many Americans, too, have begun to weigh the nature of an alliance which was less than fully supportive during the Vietnamese War. These issues tend to smolder long after the events that caused them have passed into history. In Tennessee, and I believe in other parts of this country, an ally is an ally. There are no geographical boundaries. A blow suffered by one in one place is a blow suffered by all in every place.

NATO is still the keystone of Europe's defense, and the underbrush of its confusion about purpose and action must be cleared away if the grand design is not to wash away like the castle in the sand. Neither the United States nor our European allies can afford such an outcome; indeed, some may say that even raising it as a possibility can contribute to further misunderstanding. But in a time in which there is no margin for error as to the calculus of unfriendly power, frankness is compelling in the discourse among friends. Too many beliefs that were long-taken-for-granted principles for action have been relegated as embarrassing myth to "the junk yard of history" or discarded as jargon of the cold war. It is quite true that a great many things have changed since Winston Churchill invoked the Iron Curtain as the symbol of all that separated the West from the Soviet System. Not all of them have been for the better.

We have, we allies, come to take each other for granted. The United States, once the supplier of food and capital, as well as arms and protection, now has its hands full with its own economic troubles. The once mighty dollar is today a "weak" currency when compared to the deutsche mark and the swiss franc. That is, it is weak by the ordinary measurement of the market place. For so long as the dollar is the currency of one of the two great military powers, so long as that power is all that stands between the deutsche mark, the franc, and social upheaval hurled from the East, it represents the only strength that counts on the scales of survival.

Explicit recognition of those ultimate values is not the stuff of our normal international conversation; nor should it be so long as it is part of the equation of judgment by the men and women empowered to define their national interests. But it is all too easy to permit the basic truth to be obscured by the momentary ups and downs of the economic cycle and the transient uncertainties of a democratic society in which the play of conflicting values is among the most important of its reasons for being.

During the war in Vietnam there was much discussion on what kind of impact our withdrawal would have on our allies. Some denigrated any possible negative fallout as highly unlikely. They pointed to the enormous antiwar feeling in Europe as evidence of the wave of approval that would engulf us. Others felt that withdrawal couldn't signify anything to our allies except a failure of will that would eventually extend to them. I don't believe there was a simple "yes" or "no" answer to that particular problem. But I'm convinced that American policy *after* the war had substantial influence in the way we are now seen by our friends and enemies both. The perception and the situation are most dangerous in Africa and in the Middle East.

Africa has been a focus of power and the interests of the Americans and the Western Europeans for centuries. The bitter history of slavery and colonization can never be erased. The success of the surging independence movements following World War II was only the beginning of Africa's attempt to assume its own identity after a long period of cruel cultural anonymity. If the world "imperialism" is ill addressed to Western Europe in the late twentieth century, it accurately described our allies and ourselves in an earlier time. And the Soviet Union has a superb talent for stirring bitter hatreds based on the actions of a century ago. This cruelest imperialist power of our age has too often succeeded in taking a nineteenth-century label and effectively sticking it on the Western democracies of today. For whatever reason, we have not been nearly as efficient in bringing home the reality of Soviet tyranny to the third world in Africa and Asia as they have been successful in tarring us with our own past.

The threat from the Soviet Union is obvious for all who care to see. Their Cuban mercenaries have moved into Africa to fight alongside revolutionary forces against the status quo and against liberation armies determined to maintain political and economic choices for themselves. The Soviets have filled a vacuum of power; it is a vacuum for which the United States government must bear responsibility. I believe that when the Ford administration asked Congress to commit funds to aid the pro-Western rebels led by Holden Roberto we had arrived at the point of decision. Unfortunately, wearied by the Vietnamese War, and in the mood to turn away, Congress rejected a request for $20 million to supply the Frelimo guerrillas with the arms they needed to fend off the Cubans.

I remember a meeting in the minority leader's office when Hugh Scott was there, and Henry Kissinger was secretary of state. Henry was virtually pleading with the Senate not to cut off aid to Angola. About fifty senators crowded into the room. Kissinger pleaded his case with great force. Standing there, listening to the conversation as I looked out over the Mall to the Washington Monument, it occurred to me that what Henry was saying was falling on deaf ears. Nobody was convinced. Congress had been traumatized by the experience in Vietnam. The thought ran through my mind as I listened to the murmurs in the background that the price for Vietnam was even greater than the 50,000 casualties and the $100 billion we had spent; that a loss of spirit and strength and determination were reflected in the badgering tone of many of the senators at the meeting. They were seized by self-doubt, and it might be a long time before we would restore the confidence in ourselves and the strength in the presidency that we need in hard times. I watched Kissinger being harassed by those senators and it was clear that they were responding to a mood that had set in all over the country. We paid a heavy price for what we did and what we did not do in Vietnam.

Aid for Angola was just one of many such requests to be spurned. The President was left without the tools to protect the national interest. Today in Angola, and in Cambodia, the forces in control of substantially important territory are the forces of those in alliance with our sworn adversaries. They are armed by Soviet Russia and its Eastern European satellites; they are in Angola, in Afghanistan, and in Ethiopia. In Cambodia one repressive Communist regime has been replaced by another in the aftermath of Western withdrawal, and self-genocide has been followed hard on by mass starvation. If those Marxist cadres are the inheritors of the earth, they are building one that won't be worth having for their own people, or for those who come under their influence or rule.

All around the globe we see the same pattern. The names of the locations change; the significance and the value of the territory shifts; but one element in the geopolitical struggle has remained the same since 1975. The United States takes no initiatives. The United States responds hesitantly, or the United States doesn't respond at all.

The Iranian tragedy has unfolded in an ambience in which the President of the United States has lost control of events. If the Congress inhibited effective action in the last years of the Ford administration, a Democratic President has completed the work of retreat from American responsibility in the world.

Twice in these last years American ambassadors have been murdered at their posts: hostages have been taken and an embassy in the capital of a country to whom we supply military and economic aid has been razed. An American President, in response, sent a message of thanks to the president of Pakistan for sending troops to rescue our diplomats. No mention was made of the five-hour delay in dispatching the rescue forces; and, only twenty-four hours later, that same recipient of American aid broadcast an international radio message condemning the United States for considering military intervention if the American hostages in Iran were harmed. All of these events (others will already have taken place by the time these words are read) could not have occurred in a world in which American authorities were determined to exercise our strength in such a way as to eliminate the conditions that encouraged them.

All of these events occurred, too, in one place in the world on which American industrial capacity is dependent.

The Middle East is, in some ways, the lifeblood of the American economy. Accommodating ourselves to the governments of that area in order to maintain access to their oil is a reasonable response to reality. But when that accommodation is accompanied by a refusal to engage covert Soviet aggression, when it is slowly eroded into an acceptance of a price structure totally unrelated to economic reality, when it involves submission to blackmail, respect for American strength of will dwindles at a far greater pace than our reserves of oil. The Persian Gulf states no longer regard the United States as a bulwark of safety against Soviet expansionism. When the war between the Soviet satellite in South Yemen and Yemen occurred, the Saudi Arabians looked for a demonstration of American determination to prevent a change in the balance of power. What they got was a flyby of a squadron of *unarmed* American aircraft and an announcement that a warship was setting sail for the Indian Ocean. The warship, too, might as well have been unarmed, because it turned around before it got halfway to the gulf and scurried back to Asian waters.

It is difficult to remember that as recently as 1977 the United States exercised great influence in the area around the Horn of Africa. Ethiopia, a country bordering the Red Sea and immediately adjacent to the Gulf of Aden, was a long-time friend. That narrow strip of water, along with the Persian Gulf, is literally the liquid lifeline through which 40 percent of our oil must pass. Saudi Arabia, the Arab emirates, and all of the other oil-producing countries in the Middle East rely on the freedom of these narrow bodies of water to sustain the traffic of fuel to the West.

But in 1980, Ethiopia is a Russian satellite; Iran, brooding along the Persian Gulf, is more hostile to the West than any other country in the world; and neighboring Pakistan has put increasing distance between itself and its American connection.

After the fiasco of the wandering warship the United States attempted again to bolster the Republic of Yemen with military supplies for its defense against Soviet-backed South Yemen. Both of those countries are just across the gulf from Ethiopia. Acting in concert, they have the capacity to cut off all oil supplies. What were the results of our belated decision to protect ourselves? In an almost comic-strip maneuver, both southern and northern Yemen began to purchase increasing amounts of military equipment from the U.S.S.R. Our short-lived alliance of convenience ended in another Russian triumph.

The brutal invasion of Afghanistan in the closing days of 1979 offers the most blatant illustration of the gulf that separates American purpose and intent from Russia's determination to expand its imperial power. The Soviet response to an opportunity to impose its will and extend its writ closer to our fuel lifelines is a staggering contrast to the behavior of the administration when confronted with the terrorist kidnaping of our diplomats.

The Afghan invasion of 1979 was one of the most serious events since the earliest and coldest days of the cold war in the late 1940's. The open contempt for American power and American interests manifested by the Russian strike places in perspective the posturing at the SALT negotiating table with what we can expect in our future relations with the U.S.S.R. Nothing could give us clearer warning than Russian tanks rolling across the defenseless borders of a buffer state that separates Soviet power from the Indian subcontinent.

If we think only for a moment, the scope of Russian intentions would leave us almost breathless. All the rest is abstraction.

The invasion was, of course, a reminder of the brutal murder of Imre Nagy, the last leader of the Hungarian Revolution against Soviet occupation. It was more than a reminder of the Soviet invasion of Czechoslovakia and the violent end of the Prague spring. But the important thing is what the Russian movement portends for the future. What does it say about the Russian estimate of our own will, our own purpose, our own strength? The answer is too painful to put down on paper. I have written that Russian and American objectives in negotiation are diametrically opposed; that we are not in a posture of negotiating partnership; that no matter what the packaging, the relation is adversarial in content. The Russian Christmas present to the world was a sharp revelation of the truth of that observation, and an opportunity to do what must be done in recognition of the facts.

The American people are endangered in part because of the failure of the perceptions of our own leaders. They have almost willfully misunderstood the nature of the other great superpower. Wishful thinking has replaced acute analysis. It is a flaw which must immediately be remedied.

The Muslim world is in ferment and the peoples of the region in which the Muslim faith has reached its fullest expression must find their own way and decide their own destiny without the benevolent assistance of the U.S.S.R.

We, too, must control our own fate. We must, first of all, recognize the painful fact that even the pretense of détente is past, and that the Soviet Union no longer finds it necessary to disguise its blatant grabs for power by the use of surrogate Cubans or protestations of socialist solidarity. When the people of Afghanistan successfully rose against one Russian puppet, the politburo had absolutely no compunctions about murdering and replacing him with someone they trusted to execute their will with more ruthless efficiency. Such an episode would not have occurred in a world in which the Soviet Union felt it had to reckon with the effective use of American power. The Russian politburo has weighed our leaders and found them wanting. In their view the world will soon be theirs for the taking. That has always been the Marxist–Leninist aspiration, and Russian moves accurately reflect the goal. Soviet behavior through the 1970's was fittingly climaxed with a military thrust that abandoned all pretext as to the rule of law, and forced the people of the United States to reexamine their own position and their own peril.

Afghanistan is a long way off. But so is Pakistan and so is India. Yet, they are on the borders of the newest Soviet puppet state and they shelter the commerce and fuel lines on which we depend. Russian rulers for centuries have wished to extend their domain to these vital ports of call. The czars failed, but at the beginning of the eighties the politburo appears to be ready to do what must be done to achieve its ends. It is vital that as reasoned assessments of the failures of recent American defense and foreign policy come to be accepted as cold reality that the United States, too, prepare itself to do what must be done.

At the beginning of the eighties the Soviet Union has succeeded in stirring the unstable Middle East to such a degree that for the first time since World War II we must reckon with a possible Soviet-inspired cutoff of supplies that are necessary to sustain the American economy. The Russian maneuvers are obviously a function of the belief that the United States has neither the will nor the wherewithal to prevent its actions.

Too little attention has been paid to the CIA report that Russia, one of the world's largest oil producers, is faced with the same problems as the United States and Western Europe. The projection is that by the mid-eighties the U.S.S.R. will have to import much of the oil she needs for domestic consumption. Where will Russia get that oil? It's hard to avoid the conclusion that she intends to exploit the same Middle Eastern sources that we have developed since oil became the world's principal fuel. Political and ideological differences are well on the way to being joined by the conflict of vital economic interests. Soviet Russia may well intend to make "oil" her newest satellite.

I believe American hesitance and uncertainty in responding to the moves of Russian power are the principal reasons that these lifelines are threatened at the same time our influence as a stabilizing force in Africa has diminished almost to the vanishing point. Through the 1970's Soviet forces have succeeded in fomenting civil war and in threatening the physical survival of black and white populations throughout Africa. Self-styled Marxist dictatorships rule some of the most mineral-rich areas in the world and aspire to control still others. Our legitimate interests in commercial access to places and materials vital to our survival have too frequently been clothed in the rhetoric of high-mindedness. I think that *direct and effective action is required to demonstrate that blockage of materials necessary to preserve a complex industrial civilization will not be tolerated.*

We have seen, for more than ten years, heightened Russian maneuvering for advantage whenever and wherever the Kremlin has thought it could get away with it. The history of these past years has given the Russian rulers reason to believe that they can get away with it almost anytime they choose to do so. It is that erosion of the American position that is easily perceived by our NATO allies and the uncommitted nations which must act on their own interests in the struggle that is now unfolding across the earth.

One of the most serious elements in the crisis of belief we now confront is that too many leaders have lulled the American people into the belief that there is no struggle, or that the struggle has been replaced by an amorphous "détente" with an indefinable content.

It is often charged that to concentrate public attention on the basic conflict between American and Soviet interests is somehow jingoistic and short-sighted in regard to the rhythms of history. But there will be no opportunity to exercise our franchise on the long-range future if we break the national neck in ditches that lie immediately ahead. Determination to preserve the world's most successful political and economic system may be called patriotism, jingoism, or enlightened self-interest. Whatever it is, most Americans when they think about it are fully committed to the principle. At the same time we recognize that the forces swirling in the world's political climate are not solely or principally the function of Soviet machinations, that they rise from other causes and must be dealt with in such a way that is responsive to those causes, we must also confront the Soviet ability and willingness to tamper with the whirlwind to our discomfort and danger.

Hesitancy is the mark of power in decline. If the United States government keeps this up we will take the place of the dowager empress of China as the symbol for crumbling or nonexistent power. The worst part of the situation is that the realities of international relationships would be much different if only we recognized and acted upon them. Our hesitancy is an expression of the attitudes of a very small group of Americans who have been temporarily positioned to exercise a disproportionate influence on the conduct of

United States foreign policy. They must be replaced with men and women who do not believe that power inevitably corrupts and who do not shrink from its legitimate exercise on behalf of American interests.

The war that dominated the sixties shaped, among many of those who now occupy high office, a distorted vision of America's history and of its relations with the rest of the world. There is altogether too much readiness to identify this country's declared enemies with the "forces of change." Back in the thirties Anne Morrow Lindbergh, a distinguished American writer and the wife of one of its great heroes, coined the unfortunate phrase "the wave of the future" to describe the fascist enemy that we later defeated in bitter warfare. Forty years later that cry is echoed by equally well-meaning Americans who take their politics from the left. I believe that those who exercise power on behalf of the American people should be able to differentiate between natural change and change fostered and manipulated by adversaries determined to reduce American power in the world as they fill the vacuum of our moral authority with a totalitarian vision that has already enslaved a third of the globe. The West has a duty to defend its values, to enhance its future as a living society, and to accept the challenge we have too frequently ignored or misunderstood. We must first identify our adversaries and the exact dangers they pose. We must also assess the prospects for broadening substantive and positive connections with those other powers in the world which are now waiting for the final score, and even those who are placing cautious bets against us. And, most important of all, we must act to alter the tides that are running against the West.

19

Panama, Politics, and the National Interest

It isn't easy but it is sometimes possible to take action that will accommodate and strengthen the interests of the United States at the same time it defuses the likelihood of bitter conflict with a small nation that should have little or no reason for grievance against us. In our time the controversy over the Panama Canal Treaty offers the best example of the successful resolution of such a conflict.

It was only recently that the Panama Canal Treaty became a big issue. I remember Dwight Eisenhower saying that the treaty would have to be renegotiated. I knew of course that President Ford had a negotiating team in Panama, as did Presidents Johnson and Nixon before him. It was not something I paid a great deal of attention to although I regularly signed Strom Thurmond's resolutions not to "give away" the Canal. That was almost a springtime ritual. After the 1976 presidential election I began to get calls from Ambassador Sol Linowitz and Ellsworth Bunker. Bunker was a tough career diplomat who had represented this country in Vietnam and Cambodia and other trouble spots. And Linowitz was an expert on Latin American affairs. I suggested that it would be a good idea for them to come on up and tell me about the state of the negotiations.

I had some slight prejudice against a new treaty because the issue had become politically sensitive and I had begun to get some fairly heavy antitreaty mail. I also recalled having signed that Strom Thurmond resolution from time to time. But I finally got around to taking a look at it; decisions like this one evolve in parts and stages; they are big ones and you somehow know that they are political booby traps. The first stage is to come to a preliminary judgment. After the briefings and after I read the abbreviated briefing papers I concluded that we probably ought to have a new treaty. The second stage was to examine the political realities. It was a very difficult time because it was clear by then that it was going to be a big, emotional issue. I was the newly elected Republican leader, and I was going to have to play a big role in the decision. That's just part of the job. Come to play the game or stay at home. I knew I wasn't going to like it, but I also knew I wasn't about to duck.

After maybe a dozen or more meetings with my closest friends, my political advisers, and my Senate staff, my resolve began to tighten. I realized there was a big political risk but the further I got into it the more I understood a new treaty would be advantageous to American security and good for Panamanian morale. I also realized it was a close call and that it could go either way. My political advisers were greatly concerned about that. Some of them said, "It may be the right thing to do, but it may mean you can never be nominated for President, if you ever want to run for President." The only reply I could have to them was the one I made to myself; that it was the worst possible basis for making this decision. "Someday I may be President, I'd sort of like to do that. But if I start doing everything now based on how it would affect such a race, I'm gonna bomb out with this job before I ever get to be President." I know it may sound moralistic, but that conversation literally took place. It was then that I started trying to satisfy myself on what if anything had to be changed in the treaty. I decided first that

I really wasn't going to worry about who held legal title. That goes back to practicing law; the important thing about living in an apartment building is that you enjoy full rights in it for your lifetime. But one thing did trouble me. The treaty did not seem strong enough in respect to our rights against Panama. I was convinced that we had to strengthen our right to defend the Canal and keep it open and operating in time of emergency or war. I talked to Jimmy Carter about it and I talked to Majority Leader Bob Byrd. I made it clear that I intended to formulate strengthening amendments, and that I wanted the administration's assurance that they would support them. Byrd and I agreed on the substance and our conversations resulted in what came to be called "The Leadership Amendments."

In order to emphasize how important these security amendments were, I decided to go to Panama and tell them so. I went down with Senators John Chafee, who was for the treaty, and Jake Garn, who was against it. We met Torrijos. He put on a little show for us, traveling around different parts of the country in his De Havilland Otter. We first met him in a schoolroom near the Holiday Inn where we were staying in Panama City. He came in dressed in green jungle fatigues with an Australian bush hat, cartridge belts around his waist, a pistol and a holster. The bottom of the holster was strapped around his thigh next to a canteen. His eyes were bloodshot and his hands were trembling. He was obviously hungover. The general talked to the students for a few minutes in a sort of subdued, sickly way. Then he took a lick out of that canteen and perked up somewhat. He hit that thing again, and he was in great shape. I never did quite understand what he was telling the students, but they liked it and *they* understood.

We traveled around the country together and then we flew to his seaside villa. It was a fairly modest house that reminded me of the houses you see all along the south coast of Florida: Spanish stucco with dark woodwork, balconies, and a tile roof. When we arrived Torrijos changed out of his jungle clothes into slacks and a baronga shirt.

It was then that we started the tough talking. We sat down in a little study on the second floor with a single interpreter. There were no preliminaries. Torrijos asked, "Will the Senate pass this treaty?" I said, "Not without a couple of amendments they won't." And he got a little agitated about that. He said, "What can I do to pass it? What can I do to make it happen?" I said, "I'm not sure you can do anything other than agree to these amendments." He said, "You're being very tough." I sort of suspected that the word was not "tough," but I didn't know enough Spanish to challenge it. I said, "No, I'm being realistic, and I came here to tell you that treaty won't pass unless we can amend it." He asked me if I would support it. I said, "If you do these two amendments." I handed him the two amendments that would guarantee the right of American ships to go to the head of the line in time of war, and the right of American forces to keep the Canal open against *any forces* that tried to close it.

Torrijos looked at the amendments for a long time. Finally, he raised his eyes and slowly said, "You're trying to negotiate a new treaty." I told him that I had no intention of negotiating a treaty but that he had to understand that the Senate would not ratify the treaty unless these amendments were ratified and that President Carter knew my judgment on that. Torrijos perked up at that point. He acted as if he did not know that Carter and I had discussed the amendments. It was sort of surprising when my host gestured to those papers and said, "You mean you talked about this?" And I said, "Exactly so."

It took some time of course. But Torrijos finally realized there was no choice. If there was going to be a treaty it would be a treaty in which American security interests were protected and strengthened. And that's the way it turned out. The amendments were accepted. Panama got what was necessary to her dignity and we got what was essential to our security. The results were, unfortunately, an exception to the general pattern of foreign policy defeat that has evolved for American interests over the last several years.

20

The SALT Illusion

President Jimmy Carter best symbolizes the attitudes toward foreign policy that have brought us to low estate. Those views expressed until recently at the United Nations were the responsibility of the President of the United States and there can be no scapegoat for policy made in the Department of State and the White House. Ambassador Young spoke for the President when he seemed to set a new direction for America in his readiness to accept Cuban troops in Africa as "a calming influence" and in his rejection of free elections in Zimbabwe–Rhodesia because the Communist guerrilla forces outside the country refused to participate.

The State Department is a huge institution, but when it is doing its job well, it accurately reflects the personality and intentions of the secretary. That hasn't always been the case. There are, of course, profound differences between the last two secretaries, Henry Kissinger and Cyrus Vance. They are both my friends and the differences in their personalities are instructive.

People think of Kissinger as a professor, an educator. But he is, first and foremost, a diplomat. Some say he's a diplomat from another century, usually meaning the nineteenth; but maybe it's the twenty-first! I think he was an extraordinary and historic secretary of state. There's probably a good argument to be made that he is either ahead of or behind his times; but he has enough creative conflict in his manner and technique that no one can ever take either Henry's personality or Kissinger, the diplomatic magician, for granted.

While Cy Vance has had considerable experience at the international bargaining table he is primarily a careful, skillful, and successful lawyer, and he treats the State Department in the way of a secure senior partner. But no matter who holds the portfolio of secretary of state, the foreign policy deck is dealt by the President of the United States.

The fracas over dealing with the PLO terrorists was only one in a series of events in which President Carter's appointees seemed to be trying to wrench American foreign policy into a new shape. It is the shape of a policy and accommodation to the so-called progressive forces in the world that have as their single unifying theme a blatant anti-Americanism. It is an anti-Americanism fueled to blazing heat by the sense that even our leaders are no longer ready to lead. For, until the very end, Andrew Young was an ambassador who spoke for President Jimmy Carter.

I wrote earlier in these pages that we live in a world that is not always hospitable to our values, sometimes envious of our wealth, and fearful of the consequences of our power. But we are doing everything we can to alleviate that awareness of American power even at the expense of self-respect or national survival. Certainly, an American President will take action to protect the United States when it becomes apparent that there is no other choice. Certainly, an American Congress will give support to the use of whatever force is necessary to preserve our borders and security when it becomes apparent that there is no other choice. But we have reached a point when that choice is itself slipping from our grasp. We no longer have any margin for error in judging when and how to act.

The drama of our confusion of value and uncertainty of purpose is best exemplified in the debate on strategic arms limitation and the furor that has surrounded it. The prospect of nuclear shadow beggars the human imagination. Ever since Hiroshima the shadow of conflagration has dominated the way nations think and act. The effects of that concern have had some unexpected and startling consequences.

One of the underlying premises of American strategic thinking has been the fundamental assumption that nuclear war is all but unthinkable. The huge arsenal of weaponry aimed at the Soviet Union and the reciprocal attack systems designed to blow up our own weapons and, perhaps, our major cities have been perceived by American policymakers as deterrents to war. In a world in which the relations between the two super powers are colored by mutual distrust such an attack system has seemed the only way to ward off the threat of violent aggression in almost any part of the world. But the psychological impact of nuclear weaponry as the center of our strategic defense has been enormous. The weapons' cost, the horrific impact of even the possibility of their actual use, the questionable value of survival after a nuclear attack have had the cumulative and desirable effect, in this country, of a passionate commitment to defusing their potential horror. The steps to that end have been slow but persistent. And, at the beginning of the Strategic Arms Limitation Treaty talks, it appeared that for the first time we were on the way to dismantling monsters that threatened the universe simply by their existence. But that's not the way it turned out. The arms ceilings negotiated in SALT I were simply a framework for future action; not one ton less of explosive power was available as a result of SALT I; and now, as a result of SALT II, the treaty negotiated and signed by the President in 1979, the United States is asked by its own leaders to accept a position of strategic inferiority to the Soviet Union. Such a development is staggering to the imagination, as are the underlying attitudes that have brought it about.

In early 1977, when the President first came to Washington, he proposed an entirely new framework for SALT negotiations. His laudable intention was to make deep cuts in the nuclear arsenal of both of the negotiating partners. And, in their innocence, the new boys in town hadn't used the back channels of communication to make private inquiries about Soviet attitudes to a public challenge. They apparently expected a positive Soviet response.

It was a classic case of negotiating from the pulpit. And the President failed to remember that the Soviet politburo membership was in a much different congregation. The *nyet* was loud and clear; worse, the administration's reaction was an early indicator of its tendency to buckle whenever pressure was applied. Rebuffed by the Russians, the White House and State Department went back to square one; after months of haggling they came home with a treaty that not only fails to reduce nuclear arms, but imposes a set of ceilings on various weapons systems that assure the Soviet Union of the ability to reduce our land-based missiles to rubble by the mid-1980's. The State Department and its allies in the administration must of course deny that such is the case. But a look at the facts can lead to only one conclusion. Salt II is a disaster for the deterrent effect of our weapons system. It gives us nothing of value in return, it validates Soviet strategic arms superiority, and it thus endangers national security.

The SALT process, not the treaty that has been offered and signed, but *the process itself*, is a fundamental element of this country's continuous endeavor to provide for its own security. As one aspect of that ongoing effort, arms limitation can be effectively pursued only when it is considered as part and parcel of a coherent national strategy. The administration has instead used SALT as a substitute for that strategy. The President has persistently refused to link SALT to the overall geopolitical relationship between the United States and the Soviet Union. That refusal to hook up Soviet actions against American interests around the world with the Soviet–American SALT dialogue communicated serious flaws in the new American foreign policy to the Soviet Union.

First, the signal was out that their troublemaking would go unchallenged. A classic example of that deliberate withdrawal from contesting Soviet adventurism was the White House response to the disclosure of Soviet combat troops in Cuba. When the administration first declared the situation to be "unacceptable," and then almost immediately proceeded to accept it, Russian officials could draw only one conclusion: the United States government badly wanted a treaty—*any* treaty. The presence of combat troops, of course, was only one of many such probes around the world. But the Russians had learned that if they were patient and persistent they would get a treaty, *the* treaty, that they desired. This administration's failure to establish linkage between SALT and the overall Russo–American relationship was a fatal flaw not only in the formulation of foreign policy but in the negotiating process itself.

Although the SALT process cannot serve as a substitute for U.S. determination and efforts to maintain the military balance vis-à-vis Soviet forces, it should at least facilitate the preservation of stability and equality between the two powers. The risks and benefits of the SALT treaty can only be considered in the context of the current and prospective balance of both strategic and nonstrategic forces. A treaty that leaves us with risks that could have been mitigated through SALT negotiations, and should have been mitigated by the defense programs the administration has canceled or delayed, gives the Soviet Union significant political leverage that they have not yet enjoyed even in the years between 1976 and 1979.

The relative decline in the strength of United States conventional arms and the steady and continued Soviet conventional military buildup gives this particular issue a dramatic significance. The years since 1976, and the months of pressure on behalf of ratification of the SALT II Treaty, must have added considerably to Soviet resolve to expand its spheres of influence in every part of the world. At our invitation, the Soviet Union can keep pushing, keep challenging, keep upping the ante.

Since SALT II began late in 1972 there has been a consensus that an eventual agreement should meet at least two basic criteria. A SALT treaty must be equitable and it must be verifiable. Other criteria also have been stressed by successive American Presidents and other high-ranking officials. These criteria establish as a central requirement the maintenance of equivalence in a strategic nuclear balance and protection of allied interests. But in 1979 the President of the United States signed a treaty that ignores both of those concerns. To have set these obligations aside on the grounds that treaty modification would offend the Russians was a blatant disservice to the national security.

The specifics of the agreement are complex and varied. But they tell the story more dramatically than anything else. In the first place, the Soviet Union is allowed to retain 308 modern, heavy ICBM's with an explosive capacity that can wipe out our system of hardened silo defenses. The United States is denied the equal right to obtain such a system. The modern Soviet backfire bomber which has an intercontinental strike potential, is excluded from treaty coverage. That means 400 such bombers will be exempted from the count by the end of 1985. But more than 200 U.S. B-52's *will* be counted. It's sad to note, also, that we violated a basic pledge we made to our allies that no American "forward based systems" essential to their defense would be included in SALT. Under the treaty's terms the United States agreed to restrict use of sea-launch and ground-launch missiles based in Europe. But counterpart Soviet systems, such as the SS-20's aimed directly at Western Europe, were not included.

No SALT agreement can by itself assure us of equality in the strategic nuclear balance. American resolve and innovative strategic programs are necessary if we are to maintain both stability in the strategic balance and allied confidence in the credibility of our nuclear forces as a protective deterrent. But the failure of the SALT II Treaty to restrain the most destabilizing of Soviet advantages, their enormous superiority in missile throw weight, makes the maintenance of that equality much more difficult and expensive. The actions of the administration now in power have already made the burden almost impossible to bear. While the Soviet counterforce threat to our Minuteman Missile's survival ability has grown, we have unilaterally canceled the B-1 Bomber program and delayed for at least two years the mobile-missile strategy designed to assure the preservation of our nuclear forces on the ground. As a result, if we are to establish equality with the Russians in the second half of the 1980s, the United States is going to have to make a catch-up effort that looks very much like the arms race that SALT is supposed to curtail.

Some of the facts that have come home during the course of the SALT debate are violent in their psychological and intellectual impact, but they must be faced if they are to be remedied.

If the Soviet Union were to explode its entire nuclear arsenal a force with the power of nearly 700,000 Hiroshima bombs would be loosed in a fragmented world. We have less but comparable destructive power in our hands. That's why an arms reduction is necessary. Nuclear overkill's only purpose is to reduce the possibility of an opponent surviving to respond to a first strike. That means that constant stockpiling contributes to increasing nuclear instability.

But the SALT II Treaty allows the Soviet Union to build

increasingly powerful weapons at a faster rate than ever before. The SALT process must be reinforced by American determination not to give away the farm. Only then will genuine arms reduction become a real possibility.

In his 1965 reappraisal of the Atlantic Alliance, Henry Kissinger wrote that "the United States has stressed the technical adequacy of its strategic views and the analytical accuracy of its strategic assessment. Our European critics, on the other hand, have emphasized the political and psychological framework within which these decisions will have to be implemented." Dr. Kissinger reflected the fundamental discord of approach in an essay that he named *The Troubled Partnership*. Fifteen years later our negotiations have failed even the test of "analytical accuracy." And our partnership shows the signs of an alliance in disarray. The assurance by the administration of allied support for SALT II is fallacious. It is a support that has been dragooned by administration emissaries in the name of "saving the American presidency." Moreover, an unamended SALT II Treaty with all of its consequences might well be the cause of NATO's death in the early years of this decade.

If NATO is to survive in the years ahead as the principal support of Western strategic doctrine, it will do so in sharply changed circumstances. For the recognition is emerging that there is a fundamental difference in the way the United States and its Western allies perceive the prospects of nuclear war and the way in which it is seen by the Soviet Union.

The SALT process has itself been hampered by an almost pathetic wishful thinking translated into the formulation and execution of policy. Such wishful thinking could have been understood as a natural outgrowth of the halting progress that finally brought the U.S.S.R. and the United States to the bargaining table. But Soviet behavior ever since SALT I was signed in 1972 should have brought a sharp return to reality. I discussed earlier in these pages some of the Soviet actions in the international arena that have obviously played against American interests. But just as significant is the fact that this Soviet pot stirring around the world would be diametrically opposed to the interests of the Soviet Union if it looked at the world from the same angle of vision as we do. The pattern of Kremlin policy, unfortunately, reveals a very different perspective on what the future holds.

21

The SALT Reality

When the SALT process began it was contended by its advocates, and grudgingly accepted even by those who were warier of Soviet intentions, that agreement on strategic arms limitation implied a readiness to relax tensions across the board. We could prepare for another "thaw," a recognition that international differences could and must be settled amicably. At the very least it was presumed that Soviet and American strategists were agreed that strategic equivalence or parity was a desirable status for both superpowers. Anyone who believed that the SALT talks implied any such thing has had a rude awakening. The seven years since SALT was signed and ratified have proved exactly the opposite. The simple fact is that Soviet forces have intervened directly or indirectly in political and military conflicts in the Middle East, in Africa, and in Europe, with no hint that their ultimate strategic objective was anything else than the removal of American power from a dominant position in the world. But the most important factor in the Soviet aggressiveness that asserted itself in the wake of SALT I has been Russian action to improve its position in the field of strategic arms. At the very time the Kremlin chiefs sit down to begin a process ostensibly designed to bring the arms race under control, and ultimately to substantially reduce the nuclear stockpile, Russian science, technology, and the Soviet armed forces are engaging in an intensified surge of weapons development and arsenal building. They have not been satisfied with the strategic parity they so long strove for. They have not been satisfied with the stability of mutual deterrence; and they deploy their nuclear weaponry in a manner designed to threaten NATO countries while Soviet leaders browbeat them in an attempt to prevent the alliance from improving its own nuclear defense with equivalent weapons. Since SALT I the Russians have developed and deployed a new generation of highly accurate MIRV missiles. MIRV's are clusters of warheads launched from a single launcher and targeted to land at widely dispersed locations. The United States invented the breed but the Russians, again since SALT I, have heavied them up with an explosive power unmatched by U.S. weaponry. As a result, in the aftermath of SALT I, and even as our negotiators made concession after concession during the SALT II discussions, I believe that the Soviet Union is developing a *first-strike capability that can destroy the U.S. land-based missile system before it leaves the ground.* That's a first that has implications that have not been fully discussed or recognized. It is a certainty that the American people are less than fully aware of what is at stake.

When I met Chairman Brezhnev in 1979 he was feeble; his voice was low. That vibrant, flamboyant quality in his presentation was missing. He read from prepared text in 1979 instead of speaking spontaneously as he had during our first meeting in 1973. He would read a few lines; and the translator, it seemed to me, was pretty obviously running ahead of him with an eye to sparing Brezhnev the necessity of reading the whole thing.

I remember having the impression that Brezhnev may have been surprised and startled by some of the things he was reading in his own statement.

When he finished reading I told him that if I was critical of some aspects of the treaty it wasn't that I was critical of the SALT process, because I believed that there was a moral imperative that required that the super powers continue to negotiate, no matter how long it takes, to bring about a reduction in the arms race, and in the nuclear arsenals of both countries. I told Brezhnev, and I believe just as strongly today, that the SALT process must be preserved and continued. The problem with SALT II was that President Carter had been out-traded, and gave an advantage in nuclear arms to the Soviet Union. I told Brezhnev that the Senate probably would not ratify the treaty unless certain changes were made within it. I mentioned that verification provisions were of particular concern to me. Brezhnev seized on that point, saying, "Well, tell us what it is you can't verify."

I said, "Well, you know, that's not what I'm here to do. I'm not going to tell you what we can or can't verify; but rather to tell you that I will not support a treaty unless we can verify it on our own, without reliance on representations from your side." He said, "Talk to your own people. Talk to them about your satellites; your photography. They can verify anything."

We went on to discuss the Backfire Bomber, and he ended up then by saying to me that he thought my concerns were inconsequential. I'm not sure that's really what he said. I would be interested someday to talk with Malcolm Toon, our ambassador, who speaks Russian fluently. I have a feeling that Toon may have spared my feelings. I suspect that "inconsequential" was not precisely the word that Brezhnev used.

It was Senator John Tower's exchange with Brezhnev that really troubled me because it put our problems in negotiating with the Russians sharply into perspective. I or someone had mentioned that we should take account of conventional weapons as we balanced the equation of force and that we were concerned about the number of Warsaw Pact tanks and the enormous growth of the Russians' military strength in Europe. Brezhnev replied that in the past ten years "we [meaning the Russians] have not added one thing to the strength of our Warsaw Pact, not one tank or one soldier." He added, "You in the U.S. have done nothing but stream an endless reinforcement of NATO military power." Tower, in that calm, deep voice, observed, "You know, of course, that is exactly contrary to our understanding. It's our understanding, on the contrary, that you have radically increased your Warsaw Pact military buildup." Brezhnev blustered, and John said, "You know, this is something that both of us can verify."

I sat there wondering whether this man was bluffing or whether he knew the actual circumstances in his own alliance. That's pure speculation, but it leads to the fundamental question of who is running that show—who's running the military apparatus?

A significant number of Soviet military experts do not regard nuclear conflict as unthinkable at all. They believe that nuclear war cannot only be fought but that the Soviet Union can win such a war. When that single fact is understood Soviet behavior around the world becomes comprehensible, and the Soviet posture at the SALT bargaining table becomes the posture of a shrewd and aggressive trader for military advantage rather than the posture of a partner in negotiation designed to reduce the punishing force of weaponry available to both sides. Because the United States and its allies have entirely different historic and political tradition from those of the Soviet Union, we have tended, at great cost, to project those values into the negotiations that must inevitably take place between the two systems. Here again, different values have produced substantially different objectives.

But the Soviet Union and the United States continue to share, at least, a mutual wariness of each other's intentions.

That's best illustrated by an exchange of stories between the Russian president and the Texas senator. Brezhnev commented in scathing terms about the recent move toward China by the Carter administration. He said that he was aware that the China tie could be an instrument as far as some Americans are concerned for putting pressure on the Soviet Union.

Brezhnev said that this reminded him of an old Russian story about two hunters. One called to the other, "I've got a bear" (or perhaps in this case it would be better to say a tiger). The second shouted, "Bring him here," to which the first replied, "He won't come." "Then come here yourself," said the second. The reply came back, "But he won't let me." That, Brezhnev said, illustrated the situation with China.

We laughed inasmuch as some of us have reservations of our own about getting caught in a squeeze play between the two Communist giants. One way or another, we do have to take account of this aspect of the "China card" when we think of our own security.

But John Tower used the opportunity to make a point about the worries some of our NATO allies had expressed that they were being ignored in the SALT negotiations. John remarked that Brezhnev's tiger story brought to mind what a German official had told him about elephants: when two elephants meet, the grass suffers; when elephants fight, the grass also suffers; when elephants make love, for the grass it is a catastrophe.

John Tower and Jake Garn, Jack Danforth and I were all very much concerned about those clauses in the treaty that seemed to imply the United States could not transfer cruise-missile techniques to its allies in Western Europe. Nothing since that meeting took place has changed about the severe disparities between "what we give and what we get" under the terms of the SALT II Treaty.

When our meeting was over protocol required an exchange of gifts. We gave the Soviet president a silver plate engraved with the names of the senators who'd attended. He slowly stood up and made his presentation to us. He gave us a set of twelve little engraved medallions of scenes of the Soviet Union. As we stood there having our picture taken, Brezhnev turned around slowly, looked me in the eye, and said in a guttural accent, "They're MIRVed." There was a flicker in his eye, a flash of mirth of the kind I'd seen in our meeting in 1973. When I looked down at the twelve medallions all strung out they looked like MIRV's to me, too.

Americans have a long history of indifference to the military, except in times of war or national emergency. Large military forces are functions of unpleasant need. They do not represent the essential strength or legitimacy of the system. That comes from the people themselves. Before anything else, the Soviet leaders are realists. They are fully aware that their regime is not the expression of the Russian Revolution that toppled the czar over sixty years ago. Nor is it an outgrowth of hundreds or thousands of years of Russian tradition. Nor have its accomplishments endeared it to the hearts of the Russian people. But the presence of the Red Army, one of the world's most powerful military forces, is itself a discouragement to those who seek change. The army is thus the mainstay of the authority of the regime.

In his book *Russia* Robert Kaiser observed that the Soviet military gets the pick and the best of what the Soviet economy produces. Russian technology may have its flaws; Russian consumer and capital goods may drag behind those of the West; but when it comes to the military there is no stinting. That is a wisely chosen capital investment when one considers the central role the soldiery plays in maintaining the authority of the state.

The American scholar Richard Pipes has written that the necessity for a large army on Soviet soil is one of many reasons that the Soviet leadership *can't afford* to accept the doctrine of mutual nuclear deterrence. ". . . It is political rather than strictly strategic or fiscal considerations that may be said to have determined Soviet reactions to nuclear weapons and shaped the content of Soviet nuclear strategy. By the mid-1960's the country adopted what in military jargon is referred to as a 'war fighting' and 'war winning' doctrine."

At the very least, American recognition of that attitude should have informed the negotiating process during the talks that preceded the presidential signing of Salt II. Professor Pipes has come up with citations from leading Soviet experts on military strategy.

> Nuclear missiles have altered the relationship of tactical, operational and strategic acts of the armed conflict. If in the past the strategic end result was secured by a succession of sequential, most often, long-term efforts to realize its intention only with the assistance of the art of operations and tactics, *then today, by means of powerful nuclear strikes, strategy can obtain its objectives directly.*

That's directly from a publication of the Ministry of Defense of the U.S.S.R.

Here's another for any American reader to think about:

> The strategic rocket forces which constitute the basis of the military might of our armed forces are designed to annihilate the means of the enemy's nuclear attack, large groupings of his armies, and his military bases: to destroy his military industries; and to disorganize the political and military administration of the aggressor as well as his rear and transport.

Those words mean *first strike* no matter what the language they are written in. They were written in Russian by Alexi Grechko, who was then the highest ranking officer in the armed forces of the U.S.S.R.

Whether or not one agrees with the implications of the Grechko statements and the dozens of others like it that sprinkle the Soviet military literature, it is apparent that they imply an acceptance of nuclear war as a feasible outgrowth of the military and political situation as it exists in the late twentieth century. It is a certainty, too, that the Soviet military, backed by the political leadership, acts on the principles it has articulated repeatedly to its own cadres.

If nuclear war is not in the deck of cards, why has the Soviet Union engaged in a "killer satellites" program designed to enable them to make war against us in outer space? Even as we negotiate so-called arms limitation the Soviets take steps to improve their current technology of nuclear weaponry and to expand its horizons. Although such conduct is hard to reconcile with an earnest attempt to stabilize the military balance, it is reconcilable with actions consonant with the Soviet national interest as their leaders understand it. I wish that the behavior of American leaders charged with responsibility for our national security were so easily reconciled with the facts of life. In the past two years, the President, perhaps in an attempt to demonstrate American bona fides of goodwill, has unilaterally ceased developments of one advanced weapons system after the other. It is as though he has determined to measure national security by some other yardstick than the military effectiveness of our armed forces. The belated White House response to congressional insistence on increased defense spending is hardly the mark of leadership. Americans expect the Commander in Chief to be at the head of the vanguard in defending this country's security. They are surprised and disappointed when he reluctantly brings up the rear. This administration is out of touch with the time. And it must be called to attention.

The differences between the Soviet Union and the United States, central though they are to the question of international stability, are affected deeply by currents over which neither power has control; and the forces loose in the world today are destined to sweep over us if we fail to move to defend not only our national interests but the very lives of the American people. The debate over SALT II, and the failure of perception and will it has revealed, will have been well worth it if as a result the American people take firm and intelligent action that is required for surviving in the eighties.

22

This Gap Is Real

The President's obligation to "preserve, protect and defend" the Constitution has been historically clothed in his role as Commander in Chief of the Armed Forces. But behind the scenes those forces are in serious danger of losing their effectiveness as well as their sense of mission that depends on high morale. That morale comes from adequate training, good equipment of the best quality in adequate quantities, and a real sense that the Armed Forces have the ability to do whatever is necessary wherever it is required to sustain American interests. No one in a position to know the facts believes that all of those factors are the actual case at the beginning of the 1980's.

Secretary of Defense Harold Brown, formerly of the University of California and a respected physicist, said when he joined the Democratic administration in 1979 that "with SALT it would be perhaps as much as thirty billion dollars less expensive over the next decade for the United States to maintain the strategic balance than without a SALT agreement." Only ten days later, the *Washington Post* was told by an anonymous official in the same Pentagon that Mr. Brown is supposed to run, that strategic forces would cost us *$30 billion more over the next five years without SALT*, cutting that rather substantial $30 billion increase into a time span exactly half of that projected by the secretary of defense when he made his own public calculations. It is inexcusable to play political arithmetic with the defense budget given what we know of Soviet actions and what we can see of their intentions.

There's an obvious question of how anyone can project defense costs over a period of ten years when inflation runs riot and when technological change is bound to create a wholly different environment. But the real problem is the fundamental failure of responsibility in arguing the merits of an arms treaty on the basis of estimated savings in dollars and cents a decade down the road. Either SALT enhances the security of the United States or it doesn't. If it enhances that security it should be ratified as quickly as possible; if it doesn't we should go back to the drawing boards.

It's almost beyond belief that the American foreign policy establishment in the seventies refuses to accept linkage everywhere in the world *except in the imaginary balance sheets it draws up to make a political point.* If there is one place in the world where linkage is unacceptable it is in determining what forces are required to ensure this country's security from military threat. Much information available to the government simply doesn't make its way to the front pages of the newspapers that help to shape public opinion. The obvious connection between what we spend on defense and what our potential opponents intend are frequently unrecognized or ignored; and this despite the fact that the same men who offer "savings for security" have access to reports like the one from the CIA in 1978 that predicted the passage of SALT II "would not, in itself, slow the growth of Soviet defense spending significantly." If the nation's intelligence people say that's the case why do the President and the President's men predict savings for us while the Russians go on spending at the same merry clip for their own military hardware? The American people must insist on an adequate defense posture based on facts as far as we know them.

Getting the facts we need to make intelligent assessments of our situation in the world has become increasingly difficult. The enormous destruction wrought in the intelligence community in the years since Watergate can hardly be overestimated.

But the life of the nation undulates like the life of people; we have our ups and downs, and I expect that that is so with the intelligence community. It's down now but coming back. It must come back because it provides us with our eyes and ears in a time when anybody's crisis is everybody's crisis. We simply must have intelligence, we need early warning as well as the quick reaction. That means we have to reestablish the vitality of the intelligence apparatus.

I don't mean to reopen an old wound, but there is simply no doubt about the involvement of CIA personnel in Watergate. The question is why were they involved? I don't believe that there was institutional complicity as such, but the point is that the Watergate connection led to the uncovering of a whole range of ridiculous enterprises. The incompetence of the CIA in connection with the Castro situation was disturbing. I think that, more than anything else, the CIA was a victim of incompetence during that tragicomical period. But I do not favor abolishing the CIA and starting over. *I do not favor outlawing covert operations. I simply don't want to drop that option if that's necessary.* We must also recognize that excessive oversight by Congress could irreparably damage the security of our intelligence apparatus. But given the experience of the past, it is obvious that Congress must plot a meaningful supervisory role. The best answer is a very small, compact, absolutely reliable joint committee of the House and Senate. It would be composed of no more than three members on each side, two majority, one minority, from each house. There would be a staff of not more than five people. The committee's responsibility would be two-fold: to oversee the intelligence community and to make judgments on how much and what type of information is relevant to the lawful inquiry of other committees of the Congress.

I remember an intelligence committee session when a Democratic Senator asked Dick Helms, then head of the CIA, a question that the interrogator thought had a self-evident answer.

He said that there had been allegations that Bob Kennedy as attorney general was so involved in the Cuban episode that he'd pick up the phone and call second-, third- and fourth-level people at the CIA every day. "That's not true, is it?"

Helms stared at him before he replied, "Of course it is. He'd do it all the time."

I don't have the slightest doubt that Richard Helms and all of his predecessors at the CIA were doing in every case what they thought was wanted by the President of the United States and his lawful representatives. That's why it's necessary to add to the process an ongoing and responsible congressional oversight mechanism that actually does what it's supposed to do. It doesn't mean that we have to try to shut down the operations of the shadow world of intelligence. It is a world filled with illusion. But at the same time it's very, very real, and in the clutch it is often necessary to rely on the James Angletons who have made it their habitat.

Nobody knows Angleton. For many years even his existence as a person was a piece of classified information, at least in the sense that he was related to the intelligence apparatus. But he was the most prominent of all the shadowy figures in Washington. To this day I'm not sure I have a clear view of who Jim Angleton is or what he was. We know, for instance, that he was with the OSS in Italy; that he probably had the major role in setting up the intelligence apparatus for the state of Israel; that he kept the Israeli desk at the CIA even though he was at the same time in charge of counterintelligence. We know that he had a violent disagreement with the establishment and with J. Edgar Hoover over the credentials of a defector named Nosenko. We know that he was fired by Director of Central Intelligence Bill Colby. We know that at least one novel has been written about him. We know he's a championship hybrid orchid grower. And we know that he's the archetypical spook.

Angleton looks the part. He has a cadaverous face, he's skinny, and his joints protrude. He chain-smokes cigarettes in a holder. He has penetrating, steel-gray eyes. In conversation his statements are all elliptical. He almost never makes a direct and categorical assertion. He's one of those people with whom you are never sure you have communicated until you sit down and think about it later. I believe that in the kind of world we live in the Angletons are necessary to American security. We need them, at the very least, to provide reliable information as to where to put and how to use our defense dollars.

In this last fiscal year (1979) we spent less on defense as a proportion of the federal budget than in any year since 1940. The Carter administration, slashing away at strategic arms programs on the drawing boards for years, brought in a budget in which only 4.9 percent of the gross national product was allocated for national defense. That's the lowest figure since just before the Korean War. And it comes at a time when analysts believe that Soviet defense expenditures run as high as 15 percent of their gross national product.

Even as our foreign policy-makers retreat around the world they cut back on the military infrastructure that deploys whatever strength remains to us. In 1980 and 1981 the administration plans to employ slightly more than 3 million people. That includes both military and civilian personnel. And the number reflects a drop of over 80,000 since 1964, the last year before the Vietnamese War became a major undertaking. This year the Commander in Chief will have a military establishment of slightly over 2 million under his command. That's a decrease of 630,000 in the last fifteen years. We have, to put it another way, reduced our military manpower by 24 percent. During the same period the number of our Navy's active ships has shrunk by almost half and the U.S. Air Force has 40 percent fewer planes available for combat. "Meanwhile," as they say in the soap operas, our strategic deterrent suffers the ravages of age. Those Soviet military thinkers who have incorporated the possibility of a "first strike" into their thinking have an understanding of the growing limitations on the effectiveness of the American strategic forces. The facts are unpleasant; but they're simple enough; and every citizen should be aware of what they are and what they mean. The Carter Administration's belated and half-hearted attempts to play "catch up" is a stinging repudiation of its own three-year history of ineptitude and failure to recognize the facts of international life.

Ever since nuclear deterrent became the center of superpower military strategy, the United States has organized its forces on the TRIAD concept. Our nuclear forces were designed to retaliate from manned bombers, sea forces, and land-based missiles against a blow at the United States or one of its allies. The idea was that if the Soviets, or any other enemy, hit at one of the three legs of the force, the others would survive to strike back. But the TRIAD force was always keyed to the invulnerability of the land-based missile system; and until recently it *was* invulnerable to Soviet striking power. Not any longer. The brutal and belatedly acknowledged fact is that the United States' nuclear forces are the casualties of letdown and misjudgment of the abilities and intentions of the Soviet Union.

During the war in Vietnam our defense efforts were almost totally concentrated on the needs of a jungle conflict that was not going the way we wanted it to go. The United States could make no major investments in its strategic arms. And it did nothing to improve its capacity to fight a conventional or any other kind of war in Europe. As a result, in 1980, our military and naval arms are living off yesterday's capital investments. Airborne and sea-based forces are rapidly aging; as the administration drags its feet in developing the advanced Trident Submarine it is fully aware that the Minuteman Missile (the pride of the sixties) will be vulnerable to a first strike by 1985 at the latest.

What kind of a people have we become? What kind of government have we given ourselves? It is a government that, in spite of its own knowledge that America is threatened by superior military force, has blinded itself to reality and engages in a dance of negotiation that can do nothing but accelerate the process. Instead of alerting people to the danger in which they and their children are placed, this government attempts to solve the problem by the ritual incantation of bargaining. The terrifying fact is that we have fewer and fewer chips. The B-52 bomber, once the pride of the Strategic Air Command, came off the assembly lines in the late 1950's and the early 1960's. The last B-52 was delivered to the Air Force in 1962. Half of them were either lost in Vietnam combat or rusted away under the pressures of war. That leaves us with 348 old bombers (refitted in fits and starts) as one leg of the once-imposing TRIAD. Two hundred sixty-nine of them are now being equipped with electronic air-guidance systems at a pace that will carry the program through fiscal 1983. In calendar time that means the last one won't be fully equipped until the summer of 1984. It will take until the mid-eighties for 173 of these hopefully revitalized bombers of the fifties to be equipped with the cruise missiles on which the Carter defense planning has put almost all of its reliance. The results have been achieved by the same muddled thinking that wiped out the B-1 bomber from the arsenal of the future.

Our missile-armed submarines were also developed in the fifties, delivered in the sixties, and are beginning to be mothballed in the very first year of this decade. The submarine modernization program, like the other attempts to fit yesterday's weapons to today's defense requirements, has begun to fall apart. There has been one delay after the other in the construction program of the powerful new Trident I Submarine Missile; and all of the money that Congress may choose to appropriate for Trident and any other weapons system will do no good at all if the Commander in Chief sends up signals of uncertainty as to how, if, or when he intends to deploy them. But that is exactly the spirit that has infused this administration since the day it took office, and we are reaping the rewards in bushels of bad news.

The United States has 1,054 land-based missiles; and by 1985 every one of them will be vulnerable to wipe-out before they can get off the ground. In one of the great intelligence miscalculations, or "adjustments to the political realities," that vulnerability has been publicly recognized only under pressure from the elected representatives who have subjected the SALT process to intense scrutiny. In the course of sharp questioning of the very defense "experts" who endorse SALT II, Pentagon officials have grudgingly acknowledged that the Soviet Union has increased the size and quality of its nuclear strike force at a rate and speed that was totally unexpected by American defense planning. The secretary of defense himself has admitted that Russian warheads will be able to cripple "most minuteman silos in the early 1980's." The significance of that ability is hard to overestimate yet it is almost shrugged off by a government responsible for seeing to it that the projected damage, which could be fatal, is repaired as quickly as possible. Unless the United States is prepared to hemorrhage to death we had better call in the doctors quickly.

The kind of Soviet strike superiority that seems to be in the cards will be used to apply pressure at every point on the globe. Our oil supplies from the Middle East will be so vulnerable that the situation as it was only a few short months ago will look like the essence of stability. The run on the dollar (a run that has already established it as one of the weakest currencies in the market) will turn into an avalanche. And allies with whom we have developed strong ties in the years since World War II will accelerate a drift away from American influence and move with increasing speed into the Soviet orbit. The painfully built structure of containment that saved Western Europe from Soviet dominance will rupture at the point when American strategic inferiority can no longer be disguised or mended.

We have, in many ways, arrived at a point in history that is comparable to the place in which Britain found herself in the mid-1930's. All the signs of the debacle were there. Germany made little or no pretense at the buildup of her arms. She made no pretense at all about her objectives; but the results of such monstrous developments couldn't be borne, they were laughed off as the fantasy of a megalomaniac. The smugness of the British ruling class in 1935 is being replayed by all too many of those in equivalent positions in the America of the 1980's. Instead of a call to arms and sacrifice, we hear about increases in social programs. There will be equal opportunity only for extinction as a society if we permit Russian hegemony to become an uncontested reality.

These hard words must be spoken, written, and acted upon. The premises of our conduct are no longer valid. We must stare the obvious facts in the face and take immediate measures to change a black picture. There is still time to do what must be done if we have the will to do it.

23

What Must Be Done

"We arm to parley," said Winston Churchill, and so we must in the years ahead, because the record is proof that the other side has been doing just that even as the White House began its unofficial program of unilateral disarmament.

Whether or not SALT II is ratified, continued SALT negotiations intended to reduce the threat of nuclear disaster are essential in the effort to preserve civilized life as we know it. But it's just as important to keep in mind the probability that many of the people on the other side of the negotiating table do not at present share our view of the consequences of nuclear war. A power in which a significant element of the military leadership regards "war winning" as a reasonable strategic objective is a long way removed from the way we have shaped our attitudes and policy since the inevitable result of atomic war first became apparent.

This fundamental difference between Soviet and American attitudes must be absorbed by leaders and people as we continue the SALT effort. And they underline the necessity to structure a foreign policy and its support that takes nothing for granted about what our potential adversaries in the world will or will not do. The SALT effort must be seen by the Soviet Union, China, NATO, and the third world as a direct expression of American strength and not of American fears. That's why "linkage" should be restored to the language as a living expression of American policy in the eighties, even as we continue to talk with the Russians about the whole range of international problems. Realpolitik should again be a dominant element in the way we think about the world. America's moral aspirations will be no more or less effective than its ability to discern its interests and its ability to act on them.

NATO, beginning because of American drift to steer its own course, must be the focal point for an effort by the United States to apply the principles of realpolitik. The slowness of NATO countries to meet their commitments to increase the alliance's strength by an across-the-board rise in the military budget has been closely related to a time when the United States leadership has been hesitant about beefing up its own armed forces. But we must clarify the alliance's purposes at the same time we strengthen its ability to defend Western Europe.

NATO countries, although not always sharing common views on every question, owe each other the obligation to be firm and clear in their collective action when the basic interests of the alliance are at stake. One of the most dismaying things about the wave of anti-American terrorism at the end of the seventies was the absence of public expressions of moral outrage when American personnel and installations were attacked. All of the Security Council sessions (a full month after the embassy assault in Tehran) and all of the private expressions of dismay barely disguised the hesitancy of our European allies to take unified action that would have reflected genuine indignation at the agony of the United States. The leaks to the press over the past several years about uncertainty as to the American commitment to use the nuclear deterrent if Europe were attacked reflected a genuine concern. But the concern was in part an aspect of a Europe looking for its own new directions. It may be time for the NATO powers to begin discussions of the alliance's role in the world thirty years after its inception. Even as the United States encourages NATO to strengthen its arms, and its will to use them if necessary, the other NATO powers should clarify their own commitments to a partnership in which the United States military power plays such a significant role. The recent squabble over whether some of the NATO powers were willing to place nuclear weapons on their soil in the face of Soviet opposition is illustrative of the uncertainties in the alliance that have been amplified by conflicting American signals about its own attitude toward the use of power to contain Soviet adventurism. The quarrelsome discussion about the neutron bomb also implied fundamental differences as to how to deal with the military pressure from the East.

In the 1980's we can reassure our NATO allies by actions demonstrating that the nuclear umbrella is still in place and by encouraging a corollary conventional buildup in military strength by our NATO partners. The staggering increase in the Warsaw Pact military hardware aimed at Western Europe has all but been ignored in the context of American military activity. If our partners wonder why tens of thousands of Russian tanks and hundreds of divisions of Warsaw Pact troops are marshaled on the borders of Central Europe at the same time the United States dismantles its nuclear effectiveness and marks time in increasing the strength of its conventional land and sea arms, they wonder, too, about a treaty that makes Soviet nuclear superiority a virtual certainty for at least the next five years; and they wonder most of all why the administration and its allies insist on expressions of support for SALT II by the very NATO leaders who are so uneasy about its content. Much of that uneasiness will be erased when there is visible evidence that the United States is again prepared to assert its interests whenever and wherever they are threatened. We must act to repeal a good deal of self-inflicted damage.

As a symbol of our renewed will and capacity to act when action is called for, an American "first brigade" should be trained, equipped, and moved into place as soon as possible. "No more Irans" must galvanize a technologically sound and battle-ready American force available to respond in lightning strokes to lightning strikes. Its principal purpose would be to avoid the need for its use.

American foreign policy is closely linked to what our armed forces are able to do to preserve national security. The assaults on American installations that marked the last years of the seventies prefigure an increasing surge of hostility that must be acknowledged and effectively defused. It is time to make firm policy and back it up with the ability and the wherewithal to take firm action. In the years before World War II America's attempts to build a two-ocean navy ended in the destruction of its surface fleet at Pearl Harbor. We had to start from scratch. In the age of the missile and the supersonic weaponry there won't be any scratch to start from. The morale and the ability of institutions almost destroyed by the Vietnamese War and its aftermath of psychological retreat must be restored immediately. American interests, like it or not, extend all over the globe. If this country is shut out from participation in commerce or political dialogue with authorities anywhere in the world it should be recognized for what it is: a defeat for the United States and a building block in the edifice of expanding Soviet influence.

We have just been through a period in which it was fashionable to spurn the role of "world policeman," to emphasize the limitations on what we could do to protect our values and the safety of our people abroad, and to indulge in the romantic cry of "Come home, America." I say it's time to end the guilt trip.

In the twentieth century, in which men have learned to probe space (and how often have you heard our leaders talk about that recently?), people can't and won't accept a condition in which the continental boundaries of the United States can be turned into a prison of fear by enemies abroad or by impotent and fearful leaders at home. We have always fought for freedom of the seas; and in our time when continents are literally islands, freedom must be a reality everywhere in the world.

The next President of the United States, after close consultation with his military leaders, and after discussion with the major American constituencies, must address the nation and the world with a new national conception of what and where America's international interests are. I propose that the new President explicitly state that those interests will be defended, if necessary, by American arms; and I propose that his expression of national will be backed up by the increased military force and the improved American technology necessary to implement it.

We must renew our rusting strength after a period in which an American President has resisted meaningful increases in the defense budget. We must have the capacity to put American troops where they are needed in sufficient numbers and with sufficient power to fulfill any mission they must undertake. We must have a navy with the capacity to defend the American energy lifeline until we have substantially reduced our need for foreign sources of fuel. Until that day arrives we must behave in such a way that our friends who supply us with that energy understand that we will protect them and ourselves from any attempt to shut this country down. Teddy Roosevelt once said it: "Walk softly and carry a big stick." In recent years we have walked on egg shells, and very softly; but no one believes that we have a big stick that we dare to use.

It can be argued that explicit definition of American interests may mislead other world powers. In 1950, Dean

Acheson left out South Korea from a discussion of our obligations. The North Koreans immediately invaded and we went through three years of war to protect South Korea. I suggest that we simply make it clear that in the 1980's our interests in the resources that sustain industrial society are worldwide, and that the introduction of armed forces from outside a nation's borders by Soviet imperialism or its agents will be met with resistance whenever we deem it a threat to our interests. We must, in other words, restore the view that once was taken for granted. The United States will do what is necessary to protect its interests and the survival of its friends and allies. Such commitments were recently spurned as the vestiges of the past. But most Americans are now roused to an awareness that there is simply no way we can shake off the responsibility of our past and the obligations of the future if we wish to avoid disappearing down Lenin's dustbin of history. There is no margin for error.

Part V

America in the Eighties

24

The *Mayflower* Adventure

I'm a politician, not a poet, and certainly not a dreamer. But I've just returned from Puerto Rico, 1,500 miles from the U.S. mainland, and now I'm back in Huntsville, Tennessee. During the flight I thought a good deal about these next years and what we can accomplish as they go by. I thought, too, about my days in Puerto Rico. I'm home to celebrate the new year. But I was at home there, too; in a way these pages have been about that extraordinary miracle that makes an American at home over so broad a span of continental mass and even at places across the sea which are also stamped "made in America."

I have written much here about the shortcomings of our government, and much about how the margin for error in the way we conduct our affairs has vanished from the calculus of power. I've attempted to offer some solutions to the problems that confront us in the closing years of the twentieth century, and I hope that implicit in the discussion has been the rock-bottom certainty that the struggle is worth it because the prize is the preservation of an extraordinary civilization. If the American people face unparalleled difficulties in the way they govern themselves, they also have opportunities that would have staggered the imaginations of those who have come before us.

It's important to remember that a nation is its people. The way they govern themselves is simply a mechanism to allow them to go about their individual affairs. It is the people, and what they expect of the future, how they feel about their lives and the lives of their children, that make the political process a worthwhile enterprise.

We have discussed the marketplace, and private enterprise, and national security as concepts related to a particular kind of civilization on the eve of transition to a different kind of world and even a different kind of universe. There is nothing more exciting in the human experience than to live in the midst of change and to have a hand in shaping it. All of us living now have that opportunity. There's no way we can avoid it. We can, however, make sure that we welcome it as a measure of the reason for our presence on earth; and we can make certain that we do our best to live up to the possibilities before us.

It's apparent to those who have come this far with me that I believe that the institutions we have shaped to govern ourselves need considerable adjustment. That's not because anyone has deliberately set out to sabotage our institutions or to hurt the Republic. It is because human beings make progress in different areas of their lives at different rates of speed and success.

We Americans have produced the world's most impressive technology. We have created the materials for human enterprise on a scale that can bind together the entire human community; but our institutions of government haven't kept pace with the technology; and, more important, our governors haven't kept pace with its implications.

In the future there is an enormous potential for eliminating hunger wherever it exists. American agriculture and the basic science that has revolutionized its methods can do whatever is required if the American people want it that way. We, or our children, can tap the waters of the ocean and the rays of the sun to provide food and energy that are constantly renewable. The only question is when and how. The entire experience of the industrial age and now of the postindustrial age point to the incontrovertible fact that we can solve the problems if we set our minds to it; if we think of them as adventures in the human spirit. Productivity, of course, increases the number and quality of consumer goods. But if that was *all* productivity was about, it wouldn't be worth the struggle to achieve it. We produce in order to enlarge ourselves, our knowledge, and our capacity to further the human experience, to carry ourselves one step further down the unknowable road.

Once there were Roman legions in every part of the civilized world. They represented the raw power of the Caesars and the glitter of Rome. In our generation we have legions of Americans all over the globe. They have usually been legions of technicians, scientists, investigators, and entrepreneurs. They have been bridge builders and agronomists. If we have occasionally erred in using violence, it has been far more frequent that we have left something new behind, and something with the possibility of stimulating human growth.

I'm ready to wager my life's meaning that what America will be remembered for in the centuries to come is the staggering achievement of taking different people from all over the world and building a great civilization.

America will be remembered in the years ahead for the staggering achievement of putting the environment in the service of not just the few but of all of its citizens and of extending the view that all of man can participate in that great adventure everywhere in the world.

I'm ready to wager my life's meaning that Americans will stay in the vanguard of human progress linked to human decency in the years to come. But we have to make great decisions *now* about how we make the trip.

In the first place, do most of us share a vision of where we want to go as a society, as a group of people bound together for better or worse? For we must know that if we tear those bonds asunder we are diminished by much more than the loss of power that comes with social fragmentation and conflict. We will have lost the impetus to make new things, and to find new places, and to dream new dreams built on the discoveries made by one, some, or all of us.

We Americans often speak of the American Revolution as though it were the first of the revolutions of modern times. We link it in one way or another with the French Revolution, the Revolution of 1848, the Russian Revolution, and the literally dozens of revolutions that have boiled over within the past generation. But the real revolutionary secret is that we are a most unrevolutionary people. We fought a war for independence; but we kept the body politic live as an entity. The shared values that brought us into conflict with Great Britain actually evolved from our British heritage; and in the two centuries since, most of the people who have come from Europe, Africa, and Asia to make the American experiment have come to share those same values. They put on, voluntarily, the bonds of Americanism; not so much as a political faith but as an attitude toward what life is all about. No one knows specifically where that common adventure will take us in the 1980's. But I'd like to make a few guesses and a few suggestions as to what directions would be most fruitful for a people with a long tradition of adventure.

In the first instance, remember that we Americans are the product of a journey; that those times in our history that have been most precious to us as heritage, and precursor of the kind of future we envision as the embodiment of successful human endeavor, have been those periods when we were literally embarked on the quest for the unknown. We have, albeit unconsciously, been a nation in search of the Grail. And we have repeatedly found it.

When those first sailing ships set out on an unsteady course for Massachusetts and Virginia with cargoes of bewildered colonists aboard, it was the first stage of that American journey. All of those who followed had their own *Mayflower* stories to tell. Whether they fled the Irish potato famine in the 1840's, the oppression of the European monarchies of the same period, whether they crossed in crowded and beastly slave ships at the beginning of the eighteenth century, or in the dank holds of steerage on the great steamers from Italy and Russia and Poland at the beginning of the twentieth century, they were all on the *Mayflower* adventure. They were all coming to their own private vision of America; many of the visions were different and some were of sorrow and damnation. But they all had one unbreakable thread in common. They were venturing into the unknown. If the journey ended in bitterness and tragedy for the slaves, for most of the others and for the children of all of them, it was a trip worth taking. And it was a trip that wouldn't be over until the great covered wagons, preceded by hunters and trappers, slowly and inexorably crossed the continent in a huge, cumbersome, plodding caravan, leaving seeds and sheaves of settlement in every part of the continent that became the United States of America.

Journeys like the American journey never come to an end. They have their meaning in themselves. That's why I regret the sleep that has overtaken our governors and too many of our citizens about the journey into the universe.

How the race for space began is no longer important. What is important, as far as I can see, is that when the peoples of the future, wherever they may be, think of our time they will think of that stage of the American journey that began the search for the universe. I propose that we renew the journey consciously and with every intention that it become a central national goal to achieve significant progress in the 1980's. The Age of Discovery is remembered for Christopher Columbus and Ferdinand Magellan. The domestic crises and the religious wars of that period pale into insignificance when they are placed against the magnificent achievement that was crowned with the discovery of America. But that discovery was a fraction of the discovery of the entire world in which human beings live and work today. Humanity released itself from much of its fear of the unknown when it ventured across the great oceans of the world.

In our time, we Americans took the first steps on an even greater journey into space. The literally marvelous increase in scientific knowledge about space, the multitude of universes beyond our ken, and the relation of our earth to the countless planets and stars raises far more fundamental questions than it provides answers. But it is clear that we human beings are catalytic agents for change in that outer darkness that we have just begun to probe.

I remember, back in the 1950's, a considerably more innocent time in some ways, when CBS ran a series of interesting science programs called *Conquest of Space*. No network executive would dream of calling such a program by that title in the 1980's. We men and women of the late twentieth century know that we are not going to conquer space. But we can find out a little more about it; and, in so doing, we can find out a good deal more about ourselves. The hesitancy to continue the journey is a betrayal of the best in the American spirit. I believe it reflects some of the same hesitancy that has diminished the national will in the aftermath of the war in Asia and the Watergate scandals. We must begin again.

The technicians will tell you about the wonderful commercial applications of some of the hardware they developed for the moon trips and the deep space probes to Mars and Jupiter; and they're right. There is no question about the fact that jobs have been created and new, exciting products have been developed as a result of President Kennedy's decision to send a man to the moon. But I wouldn't be nearly so excited about the prospects for space travel as I am if that were all that it was about. The principal reason for Americans to explore the universe is very simply that it's there, and that we have the ability to begin the mission. We cannot know its final fruits. But we know the hungers of the human spirit. We do know that there is nothing so exhilarating as making new discoveries and doing the work that results in practical applications of those discoveries.

In the year 2200 you can be sure that the archivists and historians will be little if at all interested in the names of the presidential candidates of 1980, or in the political infighting that occurred between them, or in the budget figures, or the inflation rate. These things are important to us; they must be, because they will determine the way we shape the larger lineaments of that future in which the historians *will* be interested. When were new planets discovered? What, perhaps even *who,* was on them? How were the problems solved, and who were the adventurers of the human spirit who solved them? Those are the questions that the future will ask, hopefully in gratitude for the achievement, although even that cannot be taken for granted. What we must take for granted is that we are under an obligation to continue an adventure we consciously began in the early 1960's.

The cynics among us tend to sneer and carp at the space program and its costs. The facts, of course, are that much of the money we spend on government programming ostensibly designed to solve the problems of unemployment would be put to far better use if it was part of a national effort that in the very nature of things calls on all available human resources to meet the goal of a move into space by the end of the eighties.

Americans, in cooperation with every other country in the world that has the will, the wherewithal, and the commitment to partnership, should have the first colonies in outer space by the end of the decade. We have proven we can do what must be done. We can let those who come after decide on the next step in the journey. But we, at the very least, have to continue on our own. The time for drift is over.

There are very practical methods to pursue on this adventure for the eighties; and they can be used to achieve the social goals of equal opportunity and an end to dead-end make-work for those who want jobs that stretch the mind and spirit.

The world has approximately four billion human beings living on it. There's a doctrine that says we are approaching the limits of human habitation as we understand it. I don't know whether that is the case or not. But I do know that we have developed, unknowingly in large degree, institutions that are designed to deal with large groups of people rather than human beings as individuals, and that we have suffered a loss in the quality of human experience because of that change in the ways our institutions work, and the numbers of people with whom they must deal. It seems to me that this is one of the most serious flaws in that faceless bureaucracy we have mentioned throughout the pages of this book. The infusion of common human purpose into human relationships is an inevitable consequence of a great national goal.

Even more significant is our need to adjust to a society in which freely functioning economic institutions, the great corporations that dominate much of American life, are increasingly involved with government decision-making on a day-to-day basis. Much of that relationship is adversarial in nature. It is the relationship between the entrepreneur and the tax collector or the regulator. More often than not it's both. The larger the company, the deeper and more complex is the tie with federal, state, and local government. Even as I write the words, I recall vividly the passion with which America's small businessmen express themselves about the time and effort they expend on their dealings with government. It is, in many ways, more difficult for these small businessmen because they have fewer resources to deal with the federal paper machine. In earlier chapters I have suggested some remedies that might assist us in dealing with the problems of overregulation and overgovernment. Now I want to come to grips with some new possibilities for a positive evolution in the way the machinery of government and a self-governing people come together.

Business institutions of large size are just as imposing in their way as is the federal bureaucracy. The difference is, of course, that they produce something, and the government, to say the least, produces nothing. But the obligations that government has assumed over this past half century to assure full employment, to provide social security, and to involve itself in the education of America's children, offer an opportunity to forge a positive link for the common good between government's duty to promote the general welfare and the work that traditionally belongs to the private sector because it does it best and it does it freely.

A whole host of other institutions can be affected by a new partnership for progress to be forged in the eighties. As Americans insist that much of the responsibility for decision-making in their day-to-day lives is returned to local government and voluntary community associations, they will find themselves in meaningful and voluntary contact with "Corporate America," that part of our country's institutions most efficiently organized to implement a national mission like the colonization of space. Think of the requirements necessary for such an effort; and think of the resources America has to meet them. Think of the new and positive relations that can evolve between the industrial and commercial sectors of our society, the elected national government that sets our goals for achievement, and the community and local organizations closest to the human resources that will make it happen—groups and individuals dedicated to creating the positive environment in which citizens with common goals can live and work and study in dignity.

25

A Compact for Progress

In the eighties Americans must press forward in an unrelenting effort to improve the quality of our lives; and we have to recognize and correct some of the failures and slack that have developed in the way we live and work. Even as our technology has given us the tools of the future, even as it offers us a foundation for the journey ahead, the foundation for its own growth has begun to erode.

The country's leading scientific institution, the National Academy of Sciences, predicted at the close of 1979 that "the remarkable preeminence of the United States in science cannot sustain itself." The report commented on the emergence of other nations like the U.S.S.R., France, Japan, and Germany in the forefront of scientific accomplishment. A quarter of a century ago the United States was responsible for three quarters of the scientific work done throughout the world. Today we produce only one third of that research into the way and the why that constitutes scientific research.

This is one competition in which there is room for everybody. But we Americans must realize that we ourselves are responsible for the relative decline in American preeminence that has made so much human progress possible.

In the seventies it seemed that every time we turned

around another American was winning a Nobel Prize for chemistry or astrophysics or medicine. We have a right to take pride in such accomplishments, but we have an obligation to recognize that continued achievement on the same scale is questionable. When the most prestigious scientific organization in the country raises doubts, we have to know that we ourselves are responsible. The fact is that American education needs a jolt, a renewal of vigor, if we are to continue as the leader in an age almost completely dependent on the acquisition of knowledge and the understanding of how to use it.

The new Department of Education can provide the leadership for a drive in which millions of young Americans will rekindle the hunger to learn. The unpleasant newspaper headlines that tell us about renewed evidence that "Johnny Can't Read" and that "Jane Can't Count" are headlines about one possible American future. We had better realize that if Johnny and Jane can't count they are going to find it increasingly difficult to survive in a society based on complex technology. When we read statistics that tell us about declining scores in scholastic achievement tests year after year after year, we have to realize that even as our Nobel laureates have been picking up their prizes, something has gone wrong in the classroom and in the home.

The only elitism that is acceptable in the United States is the elitism of accomplishment based on work and skill; and our principal obligation to the coming generation is to provide them with the opportunity to cultivate the skill and the will to work. If we don't accomplish these ends the eighties will be the decade in which the rich fruits of past accomplishment begin to fall from the tree and the plantings for the future become increasingly sparse. That isn't what's going to happen because we can't afford to let it happen.

The journey into space, the search for new places and new resources, the continuing endeavor to protect ourselves from the elements and to control our environment are possible only because of the efforts made by people who devoted themselves to learning about the world. In so doing they produced an environment in which the learning process, paradoxically, has become easier and much more difficult at one and the same time. The teaching equipment is sophisticated, the visuals and the graphics are stunning in their appeal; but the spirit of mission and dedication sometimes seem to have dwindled away. When the American people know that there is a national purpose to be served and that specific skills and learning are necessary to become part of that purpose, the educational process will take on renewed vigor and the job will be done. In the 1980's the United States must focus much of its energy on making just that happen.

We can use the World War II GI Bill of Rights as a model for the future of American education. Every American child should understand from the beginning of their conscious lives that if they demonstrate capacity and self-discipline they will go as far up the educational ladder as they wish.

The doors to our great universities have already been open wide to millions of students who in an earlier time would never have dreamed of an opportunity for higher education. I believe that we must strike down the last barriers to that opportunity in the years ahead. The President, Congress, and the communities all across the country must unite in the effort to provide full educational opportunities for every American who is capable of using them well. To fail to take such steps in the 1980's would be like failing to plant the new spring crop. As new occupations and new skills are needed to move beyond the boundaries of earth, the new people who come to maturity in the end of the twentieth century must be given the intellectual strength and moral will to do the job.

Education has always been one of this country's principal values. It has been described as "a way out" and "a way up"

and "a way in." We have been so successful in using education as a tool for social advancement and the building of
previously unimaginable industry and commerce that there
is no choice but to intensify the effort. If we let up even for
a moment, the carefully and delicately molded infrastructure
that supports us will begin to crumble. The consequences
can best be described as "unforeseeable." In the 1980's we
must draw the curtain on that scenario.

One obvious example of the important role education has
to play in our society is its application to the mission of
national defense and to the lives of those to whom we en-
trust our security.

America's volunteer forces operate the nuclear deterrent
as well as conventional weaponry. It is dismaying that the
turnover in the composition of the military services is so
dramatic. Reenlistment rates are down; service people feel
"outside" of society, and many of them simply can't afford
to live on the salaries they are paid in the military. The
rewards are simply not consonant with the responsibility.

There was a time, of course, when a military career was
implicitly related to the likelihood of war. In our times—for
the best of possible reasons; human survival—such a likelihood has at least been reduced in terms of the country's
social and political objectives. The military are "peace-
keepers," among the most valuable of occupations in this
dangerous period. But, strangely, when our volunteers retire,
still young, from the military, they are often outside the
professional mainstream. Their second careers are unlikely
to afford them the opportunities they would have had if
they had begun their adult lives in civilian occupations and
developed the connections and ties to community and occupation that accompany civilian life. Because many young
people are aware of the problems of a service career, and
because those problems increasingly outweigh the advantages, recruiting is difficult and the stability of our military
forces is far from its peak. There are many possible reme-

dies. But, under the circumstances, we should tie the volunteer forces much closer to the mainstream of civilian society, and education is perhaps the best tool we have.

Members of the military forces in particularly sensitive positions should be offered the opportunity to study at the nation's best schools to prepare them for participation in civilian life at the close of a full military career. Methods may be developed whereby these service people can move directly, when the time comes, from their military occupations into civilian jobs closely related to the skills they developed during military service, and compensated on a scale commensurate with their years and comparable to the level of position they would have achieved had they chosen to stay in civilian life. I'm suggesting, in other words, that the sharp differentiation between those who make defense their life's work and those who use their skills in different areas be considerably reduced. The link between the skills needed to do effective military and civilian jobs should be tightened; and America's business community should be encouraged to open its doors in a structured way to the skills of mature military people ready to enter the civilian mainstream. The stability of the military arms will improve and the mainstream of our commercial and industrial life will be enriched.

My suggestions for an educational "bill of rights" is really one side of a two-sided coin. The payoff for such a bill of rights belongs, in a very obvious and mundane way, to society itself. The twentieth century has produced a social system in which knowledge is the centerpiece for productive action. It is impossible in our time to live without using on a day-to-day basis the staggering amount of knowledge that has been compiled in less than one hundred years. Yet, "the knowledge explosion," as it has been called, is not a Garden of Eden. The possession of knowledge does not, as Peter Drucker has noted, reduce the need to work. There is more work required of this civilization than any of its predecessors. But it is work that requires skill; and those skills can be obtained only in the schools—the knowledge factories. As our need for unskilled labor, for the water carriers, diminishes almost to the vanishing point, corollary needs for men and women to operate the stunning computers that make our calculations, and that in the 1980s will market our goods and ship them to their destinations, become larger and larger and increasingly difficult to fill.

They are difficult to fill because we have so far avoided the commitment to educate the children of the poor to the needs of this new society. We have failed to assess our needs for the future and to plan to meet them in such a way as to employ the resources of these youngest and poorest of our citizens. That's why a rational and coherent national goal will rally our people in such a way as to make it possible for an all-out effort.

A "compact for progress" among *all* of our institutions will embark on that task as on many others in this next decade.

Innovation has been the theme of America's past accomplishments in war and peace, in industry and in the arts. It seems to me that the 1980's is the time when we must start the ignition and kick the motor for a renewal of that American trait. The inflation that has dogged us in these past years, as far as I'm concerned, is directly related to a slowing of that faculty for adaptation to new conditions and the ability to create new methods, new ideas that build a society and make it work to the advantage of all of its citizens.

There can be little doubt that we are no longer the world's principal innovators when the National Science Foundation predicts a drop-off in our future dominance of scientific achievement.

Statistics tell the same story. Americans are submitting fewer applications for patents and foreigners are submitting more. Expenditures on research and development in private industry and in government are dropping off in relation to the dollars and cents of the gross national product.

It's time for a turnaround. All of the talk about taxes and regulation and the smothering of initiative and excessive government interference are simply expressions of my unease at the kind of slippage in growth that characterized much of the seventies and that must be changed in the eighties.

Business and government must in the early years of this decade engage in a cooperative effort to expand applied research facilities all across the country. Industrial parks' concentration on the potential for future products must be linked to the basic scientific research encouraged and stimulated by the universities and the government. Here, again, a common national goal, renewed emphasis on discovery in space, can provide a lasting and dramatic focus for sustained effort.

Most of us, of course, will go on living lives as close to normal as we can during the 1980's. The great adventures are always the product of millions of individual efforts made in pursuit of personal goals only marginally related to the social intentions of society's managers and the direction of our business and social institutions. That's why management in business and intervention by government are such hazardous enterprises in a free society filled with complexity. There is simply no way to fully comprehend the ultimate outcome of a collective enterprise when the results will inevitably be determined by a multiplicity of effects of which we have been unaware. For that reason and for many others, all of us must raise our consciousness as to the implications of the movements of a large society and its relationship to our own personal lives.

In the 1980's, as we solve the problems of goals and of employment, we will inevitably be creating new problems that will require new solutions. Today's children and young people who will operate the levers of a society based on knowledge will develop attitudes toward their work and environment that will be markedly different from those of the manual workers and the blue-collared, skilled workers who preceded them. New social arrangements will evolve out of these new concerns. That's why it's essential that we take the first steps now to make our institutions flexible enough to function in a world that we can only imagine.

In the 1980's the American people will have to accept the fact that the world economy is no longer an American province. We're going to have to work harder than ever to market our goods abroad and to keep the American market itself satisfied with the product of home-grown commerce and industry.

That will take some getting used to. In the seventies we were bewildered by the phenomenon of the Sony and the Volkswagen. For the first time since World War II, American preeminence in economic affairs was under challenge. The symptoms, a weakening dollar and a growing imbalance of exports and imports *on the wrong side of the ledger*, were something that our long-time position as "top dog" hadn't prepared us to accept. But like most elements in the life of nations, paradox was at work. The United States had created and fostered an international economy designed to put Europe on its feet after the end of World War II. The prescription worked miracles in Italy, in Germany, in France, and in many other places in the world. And the inevitable result was heavy competition for the U.S.A. It has taken us time to recognize that the world is not made up of two economies—one for everybody else and one for us. If we live in a wired world we also live in a global market and we're going to have to take steps in the 1980's to reassert our place as number one in the vital game of international trade.

We're going to have to take a leaf from the books of some of our principal competitors. A compact for progress among government, business, and labor must put its attention to making it possible for American goods to compete effectively abroad. We're going to have to develop new economic ties with Canada, our neighbor to the north, and Mexico to the south. There is a condominium of economic interest that, in the days of our uncontested supremacy, we were too indifferent to explore. In the eighties it may be tougher to come to mutually satisfactory arrangements that will be profitable to all parties, but it is inevitable if all of us are to grow in prosperity. If it takes legislation, let there be legislation.

The probability is that it will take the application of business and technical expertise on all sides, plus more than a modicum of goodwill. It must be done, and when it is, the United States and the adjacent giants will have put economic flesh on the "good neighbor policy." The Common Market principle was not designed in heaven for the exclusive use of western Europeans!

The eighties is a time when we will find ourselves increasingly involved with other peoples, not just in the search for markets but in order to tap the resources necessary to move out into the universe. That is a journey that will in the final analysis require widespread cooperation, and that will offer rewards for every human on earth. As our own natural resources require replacement we can be sure that our scientists and our engineers will find new building blocks for the future in the neighborhood of space.

I believe that in the 1980's the American people will respond to the reality of new technology and a new international economy by a collective insistence on increasing individual liberty even as society pursues common social and political goals. Without that emphasis on individual liberty the achievement of our goals is an unlikely prospect. In an age in which people must confront the fact that there is no longer margin for error we must hope that fewer errors will be made.

The compact for progress is an alliance of institutions already in being. It's up to us to move it toward national prosperity, security, and the provision of well-being for every individual American.

Two hundred years after the Declaration of Independence "life, liberty and the pursuit of happiness" is still what we're all about. John Philip Sousa, the man who wrote "Stars and Stripes Forever," said it best. "Americans don't like sadness and that's why I put sunshine in my music."

Listen!

Afterword

America enters the eighties as a society in flux. We are a changing people, with changing values, a changing population, and changing prospects for the future. If that sounds familiar, it should. Similar assessments have been made at the beginning of every decade in this country's history. We've always been on the move and we've never quite known where the journey would end.

The change and the movement are, in themselves, what we view as the American experience. In 1980 some of the raw materials that we have used to build the material structure of our civilization are in shorter supply than they once were. Even so, the inventiveness that taught us how to put them to work in the first place is still very much a part of the American character.

We are a practical people given to tightening the nuts and bolts on everything from the automobile to the kitchen sink. We do the same thing with the way we govern ourselves. When something isn't working quite right we tinker with it until it does the job.

The fix-it compulsion has served us well, and I believe it will continue to do so. That's why the prescriptions offered in these pages are not revolutionary. They are practical, and they will work for now! If we implement all or most of these suggestions for improving the way we govern ourselves, we will have made it possible for our children and their children to do what must be done when their turn comes.

I've used that term "what must be done" throughout this book as a reminder and a warning to myself that in this country there is no "must" except liberty.

The phrase "what must be done" has an interesting history. It was used as the title of a book by Leo Tolstoi, and then by Vladimir Ulyanov Lenin, the father of the dark system that has been our principal political adversary for the last generation. No two people could have been more different than Lenin and Tolstoi. One was a deeply spiritual man, perhaps the world's greatest writer. The other was one of the two or three most arbitrary political absolutists in human history. Each of them had different prescriptions for what he saw as the dilemmas of his age. But they were absolutely convinced that their way was the only way. They knew exactly *what must be done.* My proposals as to what must be done are intended as quite the opposite. They are starting points for action, not solutions in and of themselves.

We Americans recognize that what must be done is up to us. The only "absolute" in the American experience is that we enjoy the opportunity to solve our own problems.

Political leadership, to be truly imaginative, must distinguish between what government can and cannot do well. And it must recognize, above all, that government cannot and should not do everything.

Walter Lippmann wrote more than forty years ago that "the greater the society, the higher and more variable the standard of life, the more diversified the energies of its people for invention, enterprise, and adaptation, the more certain it is that the social order cannot be governed by administrative command.

"The only feasible goal which statesmen can set for themselves is to reconcile the conflicts which spring from this diversity."

We are a nation of many values, many philosophies, and many kinds of people. Somehow we have been fortunate enough to successfully adapt our actions to our circumstances. We have always done what must be done, today. Americans are a proud people but we are humble enough to know that tomorrow belongs to the children.

HOWARD H. BAKER, JR., was born in Huntsville, Tennessee, November 15, 1925. His father served in the House of Representatives from the 82nd to the 88th Congresses and when he died in 1964, Senator Baker's stepmother completed her husband's term in the House. After becoming a prominent trial lawyer Howard Baker entered politics by running for the U.S. Senate—unsuccessfully in 1964 and then successfully in 1966. He is married to Joy Dirksen, daughter of the late Senator Dirksen, and they have two children.